The Vicious Cycle Volume 1

A Family's Despair

Bruce Wayne

To the love of my life you inspire me to become
the best man, father, and husband that I can be
with your vitality, compassion, love, support, and friendship.
Roslyn, I'm so blessed to have you as my wife, mother of our children,
and my best friend.
I love you with every fiber of my being!

Table of Contents

Prologue

**"In everybody's eyes, I had the perfect family
and life. Where did it all go wrong?"**
–William

When William woke, he knew immediately that he had made another mistake. "Fran was right; I can't do anything right," he thought, as a crippling gloom settled over him. He tried to roll onto his side, but found that he could not move. Calling out for help was no use either. No matter how he strained, he could not seem to raise his voice above a whisper. He was all alone here in this cold, cramped, white-walled room, with only the whirring and beeping medical machines to keep him company.

As the machines struggling to keep him alive blared loudly in his ears, William thought about the last thing he could remember before waking up in this bed. He was driving on the outskirts of Charlotte, North Carolina, looking for a thicket of trees to crash into. The night was dark and the roads were empty; no wonder, given that it was just after 3:00 a.m. on a Tuesday. He swerved along the roadside as he swallowed another handful of Ambien and chased a slug of vodka straight from the bottle.

At first, his vision was clear. He was on a mission to find an area that would be a suitable place to die; but when he found the perfect spot, he would pass it up for one reason or another. The more pills he swallowed and the more alcohol he drank, the less discerning he became.

Eventually the night began to take on a fuzzier hue. He remembered his surroundings only as a blur of lights and tree limbs. The sound he recalled better than anything else was the tires of his car screeching over the concrete median before rumbling through uneven grass. Then suddenly, the crashing of his car. Then the raining of glass from the impact falling all around him. Then, only darkness and excruciating pain. Finally, he would wake up in this cold, lonely bed, unable to move or speak.

He thought about calling out again for help from the nurse, to see if he could learn what damage he did to himself in a feeble attempt to take his own life; but his lungs felt too weak even to try. So instead, he grimly willed himself to stop breathing as he lay motionless in bed, focusing on making his heart stop beating. He tried fantasizing about death. The machines still beeped. He tried picturing his heart coming to a slow stop. The machines still beeped. He tried raising his hands in search of a scalpel or syringe, or anything he could use to finish the job; but his arms would not move, and the machines still beeped. Nothing he could do could end him and his sorry existence now. A tear came to his eye as he realized the sorrow that such helplessness brings.

At that moment, he saw movement out of the corner of his eye. Though he could not turn his head, he could hear and recognized the voices that filled the room. His grandchildren had come, along with their mother, Melanie.

He awaited Fran's voice, but could not hear it in all the arguing. His heart began to race now, causing the machines to pick up right along with it, as a strange desperation overcame him. All at once, he wanted to reach out and embrace his poor grandchildren; but he also wanted to die. He wanted to be here, and he wanted to be gone. The grief he felt knew no limit.

The longer his daughter and grandsons argued, the more apparent it became that they did not realize William was awake. They spoke about him as if he weren't in the room, and the words they used were more hurtful and dire than anything he had ever heard. He longed to cry out and put an end to it. But his voice fell dead on his lips.

"No!" he thought.

"God, please help me!" he pleaded.

"I don't want to die anymore!"

"In everybody's eyes, I had the perfect family and life. Where did it all go wrong?" he questioned, as all the medicine he was given started to take effect, forcing him to lose consciousness again.

"Where did I go wrong? Where's my wife?"

Melanie

"Every day is a rainy day!"
–Scott

"I told you," Melanie hissed through the phone. "We can't make it this weekend. We'll just have to move it to next."

Her husband, Scott, begged and pleaded from the other end of the line. It had been weeks since their last visit, he pointed out. "You may have given up on me," he argued, "but I know the kids have not, especially Bobby and Cindy. You can't keep them from their father forever."

"Is that what you think I'm doing?" Melanie hollered. She could feel her temperature rising, that familiar, dull ache returning to her forehead. "You think I'm trying to keep them from you?"

"How else am I supposed to interpret it?"

Rage flared up within her. "Don't you dare do that; don't you dare turn this back on me. I'm not the one keeping the kids from you. It's the federal government that's keeping your kids from you. And who can you blame for that?"

"The warden says–"

"No, no," Melanie interrupted, her heart beating rapidly, her hands going numb from anger. "Not the warden. Not the government. You can only blame yourself, Scott. It was your actions that landed you in there, and there is nothing any of us can do to change that."

A long silence followed. Melanie could hear her husband breathing. For a moment, she thought maybe she had finally gotten through to him - had finally talked a little sense into a man who had the gall to

5

take on a military career, and then use his security clearance to traffic illegal drugs into the country he was supposed to be serving. For as long as she had known him, she had assumed there to be no limit to his stupidity. But here maybe she had finally found it.

"Warden says third Saturday of every month," Scott said. "That's it. If you do not bring the kids this weekend, it will be another month before I get to see them. So I don't know how I am not supposed to think it isn't you keeping them from me."

Melanie finally reached the point of no return and screamed through the phone. "Scott, I want a divorce!"

Scott responded, "What did you say to me?"

She answered, "I'm divorcing you, Scott; it's over. Your selfish mind caused you to put quick and illegal ways of getting money over the well-being and security of our family. What kind of example have you set for our children? Two of them are going to be men soon! My biggest fear is that they will grow up to be just like you! As a matter of fact, the only smart thing you've done since I met you is put that money in my account, separate from yours, for a rainy day!"

Scott answered, "Bitch, *every* day is a rainy day to you. I guarantee you that money will not last you a year! You trying to make me into your father got me in here! He raised you to be spoiled rotten, having to have the best of everything. He never taught you the value of money because he never knew it. And because you do not understand the value of money, you do not respect the value of money, which is why it's so easy for you to spend it on all that bullshit that has no value. In your mind, because your father showered you with all that materialistic stuff growing up, you equated that to love. That's not love; that's bribery! I knew coming in to the relationship that you were a handful, but I thought I could change you. Boy, did I underestimate the power of ignorance. Next thing I know, out of desperation I'm trafficking drugs to sustain the lifestyle you demanded. All you had to do was sit with me while I went through the bills and you would have realized that there was no way in hell my meager military salary could support our level of comfort! I loved you, and because of that I sacrificed everything and lost it all, and now I'm in this hellhole! You never loved me, you only loved yourself - go to hell!"

Furious now, she slammed the phone down on the hook. She roared. She pulled her hair. She kicked the base of her new refrigerator, denting the smooth, stainless steel surface. The sight of the dent only made her angrier. Scott had purchased the refrigerator for her just prior to his arrest. It had been the last in a long line of lavish purchases. Even now, as she looked around the kitchen and the living room beyond, she could see evidence of his last statement. Everything that she once loved had now become a reminder of what Scott claims she caused him to do. In hindsight, she realized that it had been ridiculous of her to believe that he could have ever afforded such luxury on his military salary. It was not like they lived on base or anything. This was their own home, the staggering mortgage covered monthly by her husband's off-the-books illegal income. The tremendous credit card debt had accounted for the flashy television, the new computer, the opulent furniture, and the art that adorned every room. Meanwhile, they owed every Rent-to-Own establishment in town. Before Scott's shocking arrest in Puerto Rico's San Juan Airport, the bills they amassed (in Melanie's mind) had been easy to manage. Scott had compiled them, Scott always paid them. Just like her mother before her, Melanie had focused solely on tending to the children. To her, reading a credit card statement was harder than reading Braille.

And so Melanie screamed and kicked the refrigerator again. She overturned the kitchen table, lined as it was with past-due bills. She stomped around the house, feeling thankful that her kids were in school and could not see this. She cried. She wailed. She fretted on how in the world she would make ends meet now. With the family's sole bread winner locked up, his court costs and attorney fees ran higher than she could ever pay back in a lifetime. The bills were more than three months' past due, and no job prospects were in sight. The only money left was in her savings account.

By the time her rampage took her to the upstairs bathroom, she had begun to sob uncontrollably. She ran a bath as hot as she could stand. She slipped into the water, submerging her head and blocking out the noise of the world, her own ringing head, her own desperate weeping. There is no pain here. No debt. No bleak and sorrowful existence. There is only Melanie.

When she rose from the water, she heard the unmistakable sound of the front door. She knew from routine that it's little Cindy, always the first to arrive back home from school. Twelve year old Andrew will be at band practice, and ten year old Bobby will have basketball practice until six. Here Melanie would have a precious two hours to collect herself and explain to her youngest child why she felt so compelled to cancel yet another trip to visit Daddy.

"Out of sight, out of mind." –Melanie

A year had passed since Melanie divorced Scott. As the family sat down for dinner, Bobby began to whine. "I'm tired of hamburgers!" Melanie only half-heard her son, given that she was tied up in an examination of a credit card bill she found on top of the refrigerator. By now, the number had taken on an extra digit. She reflected on what her ex-husband had prophesized, and wondered distantly whether what little money she had left could even cover the interest charges, let alone pay down the amount. She had won on a scratch ticket a month back, pulling in a little over ten thousand dollars. But after splurging on a lavish family vacation to get the children's mind off of the pain of losing their father, the money had all but disappeared. With no man in her life and no prospects for income, she was not sure how she would ever pay any of her bills, let alone this one.

"Can't we get some chicken or something?" Bobby requested.

"What kind of kid gets tired of hamburgers?" Melanie asked sarcastically. Given the surprised look her children gave her in reply, she immediately regretted her defensive tone. She sighed as she watched her kids pick through their bags of fast food. Bobby was right. This had been the fourth consecutive night of hamburgers. But despite her reservations on the idea, she couldn't imagine what else the family could afford to eat. "Oh yeah, Mom, before I forget; I have an announcement to make," Bobby announced.

"What's going on, son?"

Bobby stood and shouted, "You are now looking at the youngest member of the Lincoln High School's varsity basketball team!"

"Wow, that is great news!" Melanie replied in excitement. "I will make chicken tomorrow to celebrate."

Andrew chimed in, "We should have steak, because my little brother is making school history!"

"Then steak it is!" Melanie responded.

Bobby gave Andrew a high five and got back to eating. Andrew tossed a French fry at his sister's face. Cindy squealed and laughed. Melanie got back to examining her credit card bill. She read near the bottom that the bill was delinquent.

"Delinquent," she whispered softly, wondering why it would say that. The more she thought about it, the more she figured the reporting was incorrect on the credit card company's side and that the next bill would reflect the change. Not being taught by her parents the importance of proper money management, Melanie knew next to nothing about handling her family's finances. She did not understand that sending $25 to pay on her account when the minimum required payment was $250 rendered the remaining $125 delinquent and she had to make a payment immediately. Not really sure about the situation Melanie did not panic because she had other cards, after all. Some even had some available credit still left on them. Feeling as if some weight had been lifted from her shoulders, she crumpled the bill and stuffed it into the nearest empty fast food bag. As she bit into her hamburger, she made a mental note to remove that credit card from her wallet.

Out of sight, out of mind, she reasoned, feeling proud of herself for being so responsible.

Then another thought occurred to her. Just because that card was delinquent and had to wait for its replacement, that did not mean she could not apply for a new card from another lending institution, did it? Sure, her most recent credit card applications had been denied, but these days, one only needed a name, a birth date and a social security number to apply for a new line of credit. She may have dried up her own credit, but Melanie had access to no fewer than three additional names, birth dates, and social security numbers. She quietly looked from child to child, wondering which one of them she would use to take out her next credit card, the card that would help sustain their lifestyle, for at least another few months. It would not be wrong to use their identities if it meant keeping the family in this home and surrounded by all these things they really enjoyed. In the end, she settled on Cindy, for the credit card representative over the phone would be less likely to question her if she at least took on the guise of another female. It would make no sense to call and be Andrew or Bobby. No, but calling as Cindy wouldn't so much as raise an eyebrow.

Content now, Melanie washed down her hamburger with a long draught from her soda. She had long been dreading it, but that day had finally come when she would need to get a job. But now a new and brilliant plan had fallen into place.

"Thank you, Jesus." –Melanie

For what seemed like an eternity, but in reality was only three weeks, Melanie went through the highs and lows of uncertainty. The uncertainty was brought on due to her unwillingness to change her spending habits and scale back. She would stress, then she would pray, then she would pray again that this would be the day God gave her and the children a new lease on life.

An hour later, as Melanie washed the dishes, she became distracted by the sound of footsteps on the porch, followed by the unmistakable noise from an automobile driving away. She knew from experience that it was the mail man and that he had just delivered mail to the house. The same thing happened that has happened for the last few weeks. A rush of nervous adrenaline filled her body, as she quickly raced to the front door. She opened it, and before reaching for the mail box, she closed her eyes and took a deep breath. Melanie took the envelope from the mailbox and opened it, and with a big smile on her face, and the thought of the joy Bobby would have on his face when she bought the Air Jordan's he needed for basketball, she looked up to the sky and said, "THANK YOU, JESUS!"

"So what's it like to raise a dead-beat daughter?" –Collection agent

The joy of a new life line was short-lived. Unfortunately for Melanie, in less than two weeks, the credit card she opened in her daughter's name was maxed out. Bobby not only got one pair of Jordan's, but two, after begging to have the second pair for away games, like some of his other teammates. Not to be outdone, Andrew suggested that since she got his little brother two pairs of shoes, that he should be able to get the two pair of Tommy Hilfiger jeans he'd had his eyes on since last year, with some Timberland boots to match. Melanie granted his request, and felt obligated to grant Cindy her wish for a new bicycle and helmet. The rest of the credit card was used to pay on the furniture she had been renting. Melanie had been paying on the furniture for more than two years now, but it seemed as if she owed as much now as she did when she started.

After paying what she could with the credit card, she was still a month behind, and in jeopardy of going through the embarrassing experience of having the furniture repossessed.

Sad now about the situation she was in once again financially, Melanie sunk into a quiet, depressed state. She felt cursed, like she was in a vicious cycle or something. It seemed like every time she took one step forward, it always put her five steps back. Every decision she made out of desperation seemed to put her deeper and deeper in the hole. The straw that would break the camel's back came a few months later, as she entered the house to the sound of a heated exchange.

"But I'm only a kid!" Cindy insisted into the telephone. Even as Melanie rounded the corner into the kitchen with her arms full of heavy grocery bags, she could hardly believe it herself. The years had passed so quickly; her youngest child was a pre-teen now. As she set the groceries on the table, she drew a breath to whisper to her daughter, to ask her what the caller had done to upset her so. Before she could speak, Cindy cried out, "I told you, I don't have a credit card!"

Melanie's heart sank. She felt her face flush. *I knew I should've been more careful when I used the credit card. It was supposed to help sustain us until I could figure things out, but now I'm in worse shape than I was before! What the hell is wrong with me?* she asked herself.

"Mom!" Cindy called.

When Melanie snapped out of her panicked trance, she saw that her daughter was holding the phone out to her.

"Here, maybe they will listen to you."

"What's happening?" Melanie barely managed to ask.

Cindy screamed. "They're saying my credit card's being sent to collections. I told them I don't have any credit cards, but they won't listen to me!"

Melanie was not entirely sure what to say when she pressed the phone to her ear. She knew that she would have to tread lightly for as long as her daughter remained in the room. But she had been on the phone with collection agents many times before, so she was well aware that treading lightly would be no easy task.

"Hello?" she said hesitantly.

"So what's it like raising a dead-beat daughter who does not believe she has to pay her bills like responsible people? I'm sure you taught her better than that!" the collections agent replied.

Melanie felt the guilt cripple her even before she could respond. With tears suddenly forming, she demanded that the collection agent never call again. She slammed the phone down on the hook as she desperately tried not looking her daughter in the eyes.

For Melanie, the collections call regarding her daughter proved to be her moment of reckoning. For over two years, she had managed to stave off bill collectors, and even a steady job; but by now her debt had spiraled far out of control. The guilt she felt for subjecting her daughter to a collections call knew no bounds. It was such that she now prepared herself to swallow up the last of her remaining pride and do something that she had long hoped to avoid. Sitting on the floor in her bedroom, with her back propped up against the bed, she spoke the dreaded thought out loud.

"I have to call Mommy!" she said, her voice racked by the stutter of recent anguish. She pressed the phone to her ear, listening for the ring tone.

"Hello?" spoke the elderly voice.

"Mommy?" she said, not even having to try to sound overwhelmed with sadness.

"Melanie, is that you? What's wrong, baby girl?"

She told herself she wouldn't start crying until after she explained herself, but now she couldn't help it. The tears flowed. It was all she could do to speak the words she could barely say.

"I don't think I can handle this on my own anymore, Mommy," she managed.

"What do you mean?" her mother asked.

"My bills," Melanie expressed. "I just don't think I can handle them by myself anymore."

There was a long pause from her mother's end of the line. Melanie worried that she had offended her.

"Well, I can see about sending you some more money."

"No," Melanie said, her desperate sorrow overwhelming her once more. She took a moment to gather herself before continuing. She had considered this contingency, of course. After all, her mother and father had sent her money many times over the years. But by now, with her debt redoubling, creditors after her young daughter, and with the majority of the family's belongings about to be repossessed, she knew her parents could not send enough money to cover it all. To top it all off, there was the staggering property tax bill she had just received from the city auditor. For the last couple of years she had been under the impression that she was responsible for only the mortgage payments her ex-husband had left her. She knew nothing of property taxes, and now they had come due. She tried to plea with the auditor, to reason with him about her dire circumstances; but because she did not respond to the original notice that was sent over a year ago, the auditor was not willing to work with her. He had scheduled the property to be auctioned off unless payment was made in full in 30 days.

"No?" her mother asked, sounding confused.

"I don't think that's going to help this time, Mommy. I'm in pretty deep."

Another biting silence followed. Melanie passed the time by crying quietly.

"Well, what then?" her mother asked.

Melanie drew a shuddering breath, willing herself to say what she had meant to say. "Can the kids and I move in with you and Dad?"

The answer was of course expected. Ever since she was born, her parents doted on her. As she grew older, the tendency never changed. If anything, it only grew stronger after the children's father was arrested. Her loving father became an even more loving grandfather, and had always seemed more than willing to help fill the void financially. This latest request from their daughter would only be the next step in the natural evolution toward them replacing Scott's financial role as a husband entirely.

"You know you don't even have to ask, baby," her mother said softly. "Your dad and I have been preparing for this call for a few months now. Just let us know when you start packing, and if you need us to come down to help."

"Okay, Mommy, thank you!"

"We love you, baby girl!"

"I love you both too, Mommy!"

As she hung the phone up, a wave of relief washed over her as she tumbled to the floor, laying in a fetal position as she sobbed convulsively.

"If you're that desperate for money, get a job and get out of our pockets." –Fran

"Mom! Mom!" called Bobby, in an excited tone.

"Yes, Bobby, what is it?" asked Melanie.

"Can Kevin stay the night?"

Melanie responded in a defiant tone loud enough for Fran, Bobby's grandmother, to hear. "No, your grandparents are tripping for some reason!"

When Fran saw the disappointed look on her youngest grandson's face, she quickly rushed in and gave in to him. Bobby ran out of the house in excitement, to tell his best friend the news.

Walking past Melanie to return to her bedroom, Fran mumbled loudly enough for her daughter to hear, "The kids should not have to suffer because of your selfish ways. They are not the problem, you are!"

Melanie responded, "What is that supposed to mean?" The answer her mother gave her rocked her world.

"Since Scott's arrest, your father and I have listened to you berate him about his decision to break the law so he could support the life-style the family lived. We sympathized with you and accepted the fact that we would probably be called upon to help you out financially until you got on your feet, even if it adversely affected our financial situation. As you see, we were more than willing to do so.

"Yesterday, I received two phone calls that knocked the wind out of me. The first one was Pastor Williams calling from the church, concerned about our financial situation because you went and told the finance committee you were forced to support your father and me, and we had no money for food. This is the church we raised you in, and you go and spew a bunch of embarrassing lies like that? How can we ever show our faces in there again? You continue to tear down all your father and I have built without a care in the world. It's always someone else's fault."

"Mom," Melanie spoke.

"I'm not finished yet! When I started feeling sorry for your dad and me, we received another phone call from a lawyer representing a credit card company suing Cindy for over five thousand dollars. I thought that to be strange, because Cindy is a minor and shouldn't have a credit card in her name. So I asked them to send me a copy of the credit card application for our review, thinking that I would be able to confirm the mistake on their end. So they faxed it to me, and to my surprise, it was *your* handwriting and signature on the paperwork. How could you? It's one thing to do that to an adult, but to do it to an innocent child that you are supposed to protect with all of your power is the worst! How is that any different from what Scott did? It's criminal! What kind of monster have we created? If you're that desperate for money, get a job and get out of our pockets!

With tears of pain in her eyes, Fran abruptly turned and walked into her room, slamming the door behind her. Melanie shouted, "Whatever!" and turned in the direction of the porch to get some fresh air and devise a plan to get out of her parents' house, still in disbelief that her mother could talk to her like that.

"Flashy cars and plush furnishings." –Melanie

Although more than a month had passed since Melanie and her mother's argument, the pain and anger felt on both sides was still as fresh as if it had happened yesterday.

Melanie sat down at the dining room table to embark upon a routine that had increased daily. With one quivering hand holding a long white slip of paper, she scrolled through the newspaper in search of the lottery numbers. She had allowed herself to play the pick three and the pick five today, along with the multistate lotto- the latter of which she made a habit of playing only when the payout rose above a hundred million dollars. Her heart beat heavily in her chest, as it always did in the brief, thrilling moment before she finally found the previous day's winning numbers. In that moment, she always succumbed to one last vision of what her future and her children's future would look like on the day she finally got rich.

She would no longer feel like she was in prison, because she and the kids would be able to move out from under her parents' roof, to a house in a warmer climate, with an in-ground pool. Plush furnishings would decorate the family's new home, and flashy cars would be parked in the driveway. Melanie and her children would wear only the finest clothing. More importantly, she would never receive another phone call from a debt collector looking for little Cindy again, that somehow tracked her down to her parents' house.

As if on cue, the phone rang. Frowning, Melanie ignored the call. When her finger finally traced over the section of the paper revealing the lottery numbers, she slumped. Her picks were not even close. There had been days when she at least came close to winning, like the time she matched three. That had been a good day, a day rendered immediately depressing when she had made the call into the lottery office to find that matching three numbers on a pick five would only net her twelve dollars.

The truth was that twelve dollars had been hardly enough to cover the cost of her lottery tickets for the next day. By now, between her state lottery plays, her multistate lottery plays, and her old scratch-and-win habit, she was up to spending nearly a hundred and fifty dollars a week from the money she received from both the state and her parents. She was supposed to use it to support her children, but she chose to blow all that money on a chance to win that elusive fortune.

Frustrated, she tossed her ticket aside and turned to her scratch cards. She snatched up a quarter from her purse and worked the coin feverishly over the silvery boxes of the top ticket. Nothing on the first ticket; on the second ticket she won a dollar. On the third, she won a free ticket. But the fourth and fifth tickets yielded nothing.

She gathered her winners into a small pile and tossed the rest in the trash. Looking down, she noticed that some of the dust from the scratch card had collected on her dress. Running to the living room to check the time, she quickly brushed her dress off and darted out the door. With all of her focus on becoming an instant millionaire, she was about to be late for her first new members class at Ewing Baptist Church.

"This church helps its flock in need." –Pastor Bonner

Melanie sat in the pew, fanning herself with a church program, dressed in her finest church clothes. Her children sat beside her, looking uncomfortable in their suits and sun dress. Melanie craned her neck to see over the tall man the usher had just seated in front of her, feeling anxious about the pastor's message. She knew that soon the moment would come, and she did not want to be distracted and miss it this time.

"How many churches have we joined this year?" Andrew whispered through the side of his lips. "I want to go back to Second Baptist with Grandma!"

Melanie scolded him with her eyes, shushing him as quietly as she could. She knew that she must quickly change her expression to one of hope and humility. However, she could sense that the preacher was getting around to what had become, over the last few months, her favorite part of the service. She felt butterflies forming in the pit of her stomach.

"And in the spirit of giving," Pastor Bonner spoke graciously to his congregants, "I ask that you all keep in mind our newest members, Melanie Johnson, and her three young children, Andrew, Bobby, and Cindy."

Focused on looking as downtrodden as she could, Melanie chanced a glance at her children. As usual, they did not seem to be paying attention. She wished that she could bark at them, to tell them to sit up straight and look both humble and attentive; but she could already feel many of the eyes in the church turn to her, as they often did in these moments. She closed her eyes as she focused on not making eye contact with anyone, while making her lips quiver as if in sorrow.

A collective groan of pity issued from the congregation. Melanie could feel the care and desire for charity rise up all around. With it, she felt that old familiar pang of guilt, if only for a moment. As much as she disliked herself for taking advantage of the charity of yet another church, she justified it, because how else would she get out of her parents' house?

Pastor Bonner's voice rose up into the rafters of the church, seeming to reverberate off the stainless glass depiction of Jesus Christ just behind the altar. "So I ask you, good parishioners, please keep Melanie and her children in mind when you give to the offering plate. For where many others would turn a blind eye, this church helps its flock in need."

"Deacon Randall," Pastor Bonner called, "please lead this beautiful family down to the altar for a special prayer."

After a brief moment of silence with her eyes closed, Melanie heard a voice say,

"Let me pray for you, sister." Deacon Randall spoke while grabbing Melanie's hand. She was soon overcome by the sweetest smell she had ever smelled. When she opened her eyes to see who the scent belonged to, her knees became weak, and buckled at the sight of the most beautiful man of God she had ever laid her eyes on.

When Melanie finally regained her balance, Randall reached out for her with his other arm, while winking at little Cindy. With a confident smile on his face he gave Melanie a hug and whispered in her ear, "Don't worry, beautiful, that happens all the time!"

Melanie smiled at Randall in an effort to hide her embarrassment, her attention quickly shifted from her kids and worrying about looking downtrodden, to following the young deacon to the altar.

"You don't even know him." –Fran

Melanie worked feverishly in her parents' basement, ironing her favorite dress. She was filled with nervous anticipation preparing, as this was the day her new boyfriend Randall, the young deacon she met at church, found out how much severance pay he got from the closing of the manufacturing plant he had worked at for the last few years. If it was enough, Randall's plan was to marry Melanie, and move her and the kids to a new home in his hometown of Pittsburgh, Pennsylvania.

Melanie knew that the relationship had advanced at a rapid pace, but Randall was everything she had hoped for, and everything she needed. He was not like your typical boring, straight-laced, Bible toting man of God. He was funny; he knew how to talk to a lady. He loved to party, and he really knew how to make a woman feel good. He made Melanie feel emotions and sensations she had never felt before. The most important thing was that with this settlement Randall was getting, he would be financially set. Melanie would not only avoid having to get a job, she would finally have a way out of her parents' house.

Melanie reflected on a conversation she'd had with her mother the day before, when she had announced Randall's plans, and the possibility of her and the kids relocating.

"I don't have a good feeling about this guy!" Fran said.

"Why?" replied Melanie. "You don't even know him!" she continued.

"Exactly!" Fran screamed. "I've known him as long as you have, barely four months. How can you truly say you know a person in that short amount of time?"

"Ma!" screamed Melanie.

"Shut up, I'm not done!" yelled Fran.

"I do not like the way he talks to the kids, and I saw what he did to you in my kitchen!"

"You're just jealous!" answered Melanie, as she stormed out of the house.

In the middle of her flashback, Melanie was startled by the ringing of the doorbell. She thought to herself, *Who could it be this early in the afternoon?* When she opened the door, to her surprise, there stood Randall, her knight in shining armor.

"Hey, baby," Randall said in a smooth, laid-back tone.

"Hey, honey," answered Melanie. "What are you doing here so early?" she asked. "I wasn't expecting to see you until late this afternoon," she continued.

"Yeah, I got some news this morning, and I thought it would be best if I delivered it to you in person," answered Randall.

With her emotions getting the best of her, Melanie suddenly started shedding tears. She immediately thought to herself that he came to tell her their relationship was over. What happened? What caused Randall to change his mind? *Was my mother right about him after all?* she asked herself, before Randall yelled in excitement:

"Pack your bags, because we are moving to Pittsburgh!"

Preparing for the worst, Melanie's response was more subdued than she thought it would be. Finally, as reality hit her from the news Randall just gave her, Melanie thought out loud.

"We're moving to Pittsburgh. Wow!"

"Please take care of my babies!" –William

"Well, this is it," Melanie announced to her parents as she hugged them. "Thank you for everything, and please do not worry about anything; we will be just fine," she stressed.

"Kids, come say goodbye to your grandparents!" she called out the window.

"Good bye, Grams, goodbye, Grandpa. We love you!" the children screamed.

With tears in her eyes, Fran responded, "We love you, too!"

William then turned to walk his daughter and grandchildren to the car, while Fran, still overcome with emotion, remained in the house. Randall sat in the car listening to music as William approached.

"Please take care of my babies," William pleaded. "And have a safe trip," he added.

Barely acknowledging his future father-in-law's presence, Randall called out for Melanie and the kids, "Let's go!"

As the family drove away, William waved, and before they got out of his sight, he yelled out, "Call us when you get there!"

When he turned to go back inside the house, he too, like his wife, became overcome by sadness, and the feeling of uncertainty for what the future would bring Melanie and the kids. His gut already told him that she was making a horrible decision, moving with the children to Pittsburgh. He fought with all his power against saying anything against his daughter's plans with a man she barely knew, because he chalked his feelings up to just being an overprotective father.

William thought quietly, *It was one thing that he didn't get out of the car when I went to talk to him, but the fact that Randall didn't even have enough respect or decency to turn the music down spoke volumes.*

Sure, they stayed longer than originally planned, and now that Melanie and the kids were gone and no longer a financial burden, life would be much easier on William and Fran. But William could not help but think, *At what cost?*

"We're home!" –Randall

During the long journey from Charlotte to Pittsburgh, all Melanie could focus on was how excited the kids were to move. She welcomed the drastic change for them, because the past few years were filled with both heartbreak and financial hardship.

For the first time in a long while, Melanie was excited about the family's future, and she owed it all to Randall. As she squeezed his hand, she looked at him and said, "I will be forever grateful for the opportunity to truly experience happiness that you have blessed me and my children with!"

Randall smiled then he nodded his head before returning his attention back to the road as he drove. It was midnight when the family finally reached the Fort Pitt Tunnel. Randall, normally reserved and laid back, sounded like a ten-year-old boy on Christmas day, yelling with extreme excitement.

"We will be there after we drive through this tunnel!"

When they got to the end of the tunnel, it seemed as if they had crossed through a gateway, and Pittsburgh was heaven. It may have been around midnight on the clock, but the skyline was lit up so brightly it turned night into day.

Randall next navigated through the downtown area, heading towards Centre Avenue on their way to the East Liberty section of the city. They drove past the Hill district that had beautiful, huge homes lining both sides of the street. Melanie started visualizing what their new home would look like, and smiled.

As she started to wonder how close they were, that's when Randall turned on his blinker and made a left-hand turn. *Could this be?* Melanie thought to herself. "Are we almost there?" she asked Randall.

"Yes," Randall responded.

They turned and drove up a steep hill that took about three minutes, but due to their excitement, it seemed more like *thirty*-three minutes. That's when the scenery drastically changed.

Gone were the large, beautiful homes on opposite sides of the street, and in their place were empty row houses, with trash and broken glass all around. There was graffiti covering every street sign, with a bunch of guys standing on every corner, suspiciously staring at each car that passed.

Randall finally reached the top of the hill. Melanie, hoping he had made a wrong turn, tried to read what the street sign said, to figure out if it was the street Randall said they were moving to or not. But the bullet holes made it impossible to interpret. That's when the family heard Randall say the two words they would never forget.

"We're home!"

"If it was good enough for me, then it's good enough for you." –Randall

"Where is our house?" Andrew asked.

"What are you, blind?" Randall sarcastically responded. "Right in front of you!"

To Melanie's dismay, the family's new home was nothing like she had imagined at all. Instead of the white picket fence she envisioned, there were chains surrounding a yard of concrete, with a small patch of grass.

"Ma, is this the proj–?" Bobby tried asking.

"Why you ungrateful, spoiled little brat!" interrupted Randall. "No, it's not the projects; it's Garfield Heights, and this is the very unit

I grew up in! If it was good enough for me, then it's good enough for you! Now get your snobby, skinny ass out of my car before I punch you in your little bird chest!"

After Randall's venomous response to their brother's question, Andrew and Cindy stood silent, with their mouths wide open, as Bobby looked over at his mother for comfort, with tears in his eyes. Caught off-guard by Randall's explosive response, Melanie stood torn. Torn between defending her son from her new lifeline, and possibly pissing Randall off, causing him to send her with the kids packing back to her parents' house. The way she looked at it is, he did not have to accept her and the kids, so they all should be more appreciative. *I taught Bobby better than that,* she thought to herself.

The decision she would ultimately make surprised everyone. It signified the beginning of the end of her family as she knew it. With a stern but calm voice, she looked at Bobby, and spoke in a way she had never spoken to her children before.

"I always told you to be careful what you asked for, because you and your brother always complained about having to cut the grass, and now you don't have to. Now, apologize to your father, and get your shit out of the car before you get a spanking!"

As Melanie turned to head towards the house, there stood Randall, with a loving smile of support on his face. He reached out to hold her hand and she said, "It's good to be home, baby!"

"At least he loves me!" –Melanie

It was Sunday the 18th of August, two months after moving, when little Cindy woke up with more excitement than she had shown since before Randall entered her family's lives. Like many little girls, Cindy loved shopping for new clothes. And today would be the day they all went school shopping.

After accompanying Randall to the mall the last couple of months and watching as he blew through the money he received from his old job on everything from men's fashions for himself, to women's jewelry for his cousin, the kids all joined him on his shopping sprees with controlled anticipation, hoping that he would buy them something, only to be disappointed every time. Their mother ended every trip the same way, justifying Randall's actions with the promise that their day was coming, and it finally had.

"Wake up, fat heads!" she screamed, as she ran out of the bedroom she shared with Andrew and Bobby, heading to the kitchen.

"Ma, what's for breakfast?" she asked.

Melanie stood with her back towards little Cindy, fighting the urge to turn around. She worried that her sweet, innocent daughter would detect the stress and fear she wore on her face from Randall staying out all night and cheating on her with numerous women he used to go to high school with.

"Ma, Ma, did you hear me?" Cindy called again.

"Cereal!" Melanie finally replied.

Usually cereal is the last thing Cindy wants to have for breakfast, but this was a special day, and it seemed that nothing was going to kill her joy.

"Okay," she responded, as she turned to see if her brothers were up and dressed yet. Just then, the front door swung open, and in stumbled Randall. Not losing a step, Cindy started singing to Randall until she was out of his sight, "We're going to the mall - we're going to the mall."

"I told you next month!" Randall screamed from the living room. Melanie poked her head out from the kitchen, a look of confusion pressed on her face. There she saw Randall, kicked back, looking and smelling like he was high on something as he sat in the new recliner Melanie rented for the house. He looked at her with a critical eye and raised an empty beer can that was on the floor beside the chair and shook it from side to side, suggesting he wanted one.

Sighing, Melanie drifted into the kitchen to fulfill his request for a new can. "You said today," she called back to him. "The kids are all excited about going school shop—"

Before she could finish the statement, she felt a hand close over the back of her neck. Her mind reeled as she was yanked upright, the fingers digging painfully into her skin. Randall wheeled her around, pressing her face so close to his that she could smell the weed and crack seeping out of his pores.

"Don't you tell me what I said and didn't say," he hissed. "If I said I told you next month, then I told you next month! I don't care if school starts next week!"

The pain in Melanie's neck grew sharper as Randall tightened his grip. She began to quiver in fear. Such was her terror that the can of beer she had gotten for Randall slipped from her grasp. The unopened can tumbled to the floor, puncturing as it caught the sharp bottom corner of the refrigerator. The tear in the can caused beer to fizz in a soft spray across the linoleum.

"See what you did?" Randall said, as his eyes darted to the floor. He moved his hand down to Melanie's shoulder, squeezing so hard it caused her to wince. "Now apologize to the brats, and tell them you were mistaken about the date they were going school shopping. Then I won't beat your ass for wasting one of my beers."

Melanie nodded rigidly, overcome as she was by the grip of fear. Randall finally released his grasp. "Good," he said. Casually he passed her by, as he reached into the refrigerator to retrieve a new beer for himself. He cracked it open, making his way back to the living room. "Now clean that shit up!" he barked over his shoulder, before telling her he loved her.

Melanie could feel the tears form as she watched her lover walk out of the kitchen. Randall didn't even glance back at her as his cold eyes trained on the flickering television.

Randall was not one to mince words, Melanie had to admit. And this was not the first time in their short relationship that he had hurt her physically. She rubbed on the rapidly forming bruise on the back of her neck, fretting about how she might hide it from her kids. But before she could take the thought any further, she remembered the beer on the floor. Dutifully, she bent down to pick up the can, then she set out in search of the mop. *At least he loves me!* she thought to herself. *At least he loves me!*

"I am a good woman. I deserve better than this!" –Melanie

"Oh man, not again!" Melanie shrieked. Awakened by a warm sensation running down her leg, she quickly turned to Randall's side of the bed. Overwhelmed with sadness but not surprised, she glanced at the clock next to the bed reading 2:43 in the morning. Randall was still not home lying in bed next to her. In his place, resting peacefully, was little Cindy, who for the last couple of months made it a habit of doing something she had not done since she was a couple of years old, sneaking into her mother's bed in the middle of the night.

"Wake up, Cindy," Melanie whispered, as she nudged her daughter.

"You got me again!" she stated.

Startled from the sudden jolt as she slept, Cindy began to cry. Her eyes blood-shot red, she got up to head to the bathroom to take a bath.

Melanie watched her daughter with concern as she walked through the bathroom door.

What's wrong with her? she asked herself.

Cindy has not wet the bed since she was a baby, and now she has done it twice this week? she thought.

Something must be going on in school. Maybe she is having a hard time making new friends, she figured.

Maybe she misses her grandparents. I should have her give them a call later, she said to herself, as she headed to the bathroom to take a shower.

After finishing, she tucked Cindy back in bed with her brothers, and went to the living room to sleep on the couch. As she tossed and turned, struggling to find the perfect position, her lips started to quiver because of the draft of air coming from the hole in the plastic covering the broken window.

Her mind started to race with thoughts of Randall and what he was doing. She questioned what it was about her that made him want to stay out all night, every night, and cause him to run around with different women.

After all, he was not only a Christian man, but he had a leadership role in the church when they met. And now he is out on the town every night doing the works of the devil.

"Did the extra burden of supporting me and the kids cause Randall to become this monster?" she questioned herself.

Hell! That does not justify him slapping me around like he does! she thought.

With adrenaline rushing so fast through her body, she felt as if she had drunk a whole pot of coffee. Without realizing she was doing it, Melanie started talking out loud to herself.

"As much as I hate to admit it, Mom was right; I shouldn't have moved so quickly in the relationship with Randall. But I was so focused on moving out of her house that I lost sight of what was really important. I am a good woman, and I deserve better than this!"

"And when Randall gets home, I will tell him that the kids and I are moving out, because it's over!"

After meditating for a few minutes, she finally found a comfortable position. Before falling asleep, she prayed a short prayer.

"God, please help me and the kids out of this situation. I don't want to go back to Mom and Dad's but I have to! In Jesus' name I pray, amen.

"I'm down for whatever!" –Melanie

"What are you doing out here on the couch?" Randall asked.

With a big yawn, Melanie stretched before rolling over and asking what time it was.

"It's 8:07," Randall replied.

"The question is, where have you been, and with whom, that did not allow you to come home until 8:07?" asked Melanie.

Surprised at her line of questioning, Randall responded,

"None of your damn business!"

"It's a rhetorical question!" Melanie stated. "I already know the answer!" she continued.

"My only question is why?"

"Why what?" asked Randall.

"Why move me and the kids across the country with the promise of a better life, only to physically abuse and cheat on me?"

Expecting the worst, she was immediately caught off-guard by the remorse Randall showed as he addressed her issue.

"It was not my plan to do that to you, baby. But when I moved back to Pittsburgh, dressing the way I do and driving my new car, I went from being the nerd that lived in the smallest unit in the complex, to the most interesting man in the city. Women who never gave me the time of day when I was younger give me all their attention now! They do any and everything I want them to do from drugs to sex. They are down for whatever!"

"I love you, Melanie!" he continued. "Here at home, with you and the kids, I struggle being the man of God I was portraying when we met at church. But with them, I can be whoever I want to be, with no stress or strings attached, and I love it!"

Overcome with emotion, Melanie started crying.

Totally going against what she had planned to do, she asked, "Is there a way I can save our relationship? I am down for whatever!"

As she attempted to wipe away her tears, Randall grabbed Melanie's hand and wiped her face dry.

"Are you really down for whatever?" he asked.

"Yes, I just want to save our relationship!" Melanie answered.

Randall reached out his hand and said, "Then come with me to the bedroom. I want you to try something."

As Melanie followed her lover into the room, she felt both a sense of accomplishment and relief. She was not only able to avoid being sent back to her parents' house, but she appeared to have secured control of her and her kids' future. All she needed to do was keep Randall happy.

"Ma! Are you in there?" Bobby called as he knocked at the bedroom door.

"Go away, she will be out later!"

Cindy

"Excited about today, I feel my life will never be the same!"
–Cindy

Cindy sat nervously across the mahogany desk covered with paperwork and applications as if they were the skeletal remains of other people who had been there before her. The person sitting across from her examined her most intimate financial history. To take her mind off of the unnerving situation, she logged into Facebook to give a status update. She posted, "Excited about today, I feel my life will never be the same!" Cindy had no clue how true that statement was.

After logging off of Facebook, she returned her attention back to her present situation, and the man she had never met before this morning, but yet, entrusted him with her credit report.

Her first impression of the guy was that he looked a little disheveled and disorganized, but she thought that he had a very kind face. He also appeared to be extremely genuine when he expressed that he was on a mission to help Cindy and others like her with their personal finances.

The reason she was in his office is because he had overheard her conversation with the bank teller in the lobby of the bank.

"No," Cindy stated. "I just want to open up your most basic checking account. Why do I need to speak to your colleague?" she continued.

The teller responded with a look of empathy and a relaxed smile on her face, as if she was a recent graduate of the teller academy.

"Ms. Johnson, I understand exactly what you're saying; however, we make it our goal to treat every customer the same, whether you have ten thousand dollars in the bank, or ten million. You came into the bank with a perceived need of opening up a checking account, but it's my banking center partner's job to uncover the unperceived needs you don't realize you have."

"So how long will the process take? I have an appointment at the furniture rental place down the street at 2:00 p.m., which means I should be leaving soon."

Suddenly a strange voice interjected, "Excuse me, miss. Please allow me to introduce myself. My name is Mr. Marks, your friendly neighborhood personal banker. Let me start by apologizing for listening to the conversation you were having with my colleague without your knowledge, but I would be remiss as a banker if I did not warn you how unwise it is to throw your hard-earned money down the drain renting furniture.

"If you ever get to the point of paying off the furniture, and that's a big *if*, you would have paid for it three times over from all of the interest and fees you would be charged.

"We have the best loan programs in town, with the lowest interest rates available to you; but before I invite you into my office, I have to ask you one question."

"Sure, what is it?"

"How's your credit?"

Even though she had not ever thought to look at her credit report because she had never applied for any type of credit before, her pride led her to respond to his inquiry with an emphatic, "It's great!"

"Fantastic," he replied. "Then follow me."

As both the banker and Cindy turned to go into his office, he announced, "From your response about your credit, I can guarantee you will qualify for one of our loan programs."

"Perfect!" Cindy responded.

The interaction with Mr. Marks made it easy for her to let her guard down and relax, because she finally felt that she was in the good hands of someone she could really trust.

But now, that kind face he once had, had twisted into something entirely different. And it seemed as if he could not wait to get Cindy out of his office. As he examined Cindy's credit report, he had assumed a look of disgust.

"Is everything okay?" Cindy asked with a wavering voice before coughing, which is something she had been doing an awful lot of over the last few months.

The banker smirked as his beady eyes scanned aimlessly over the computer screen standing between them.

Cindy melted into a nervous laugh. "That credit score still has three digits, right?" she asked jokingly, as she tried to lighten the mood.

Mr. Marks looked at her with a serious gaze as he answered her with a sharp and demeaning tone. "Barely!"

She shook her head, feeling her blood run cold, as if there must be some sort of mistake. "You're joking, right?" she asked.

He shook his head no and stated, "I take my job too seriously, and respect other people's time enough not to waste it playing games, unlike you!"

Cindy became overwhelmed with both anger and confusion. Anger because she thought to herself, *Oh no, this old sloppy-looking man dressed like a slimy insurance salesman didn't just talk to me like that?* But she was confused about why her credit score could be as bad as he said it is.

"Are you sure you have the right Cindy Johnson?" she asked. "I mean, Johnson is a very common last name."

Finally short of patience, the banker slammed his pen down on the desk and turned his computer screen around to face Cindy so she could see what he was talking about. As he pointed to the box in the top right corner of the screen he asked, "This is your social security number, right?"

Cindy leaned over to read the number, but became distracted by the three-digit number in red just below, indicating that her credit score was a dismal 321. Reflexively, she shook her head no.

"So that is not your number?" Mr. Marks sternly asked as if she was a kid being reprimanded.

Cindy rescanned the social security number, as the embarrassing realization set in that it *was* her social security number. She noticed dates on the report that went back more than ten years that she did not understand, but did not want to ask for clarification, because she did not want to give Mr. Marks another reason to talk to her the way he had.

"Three-twenty-one," she mumbled, as she exhaled in disgust.

"Yeah," the banker sarcastically remarked. "This is the lowest score I have ever seen personally, and with the three overdrawn accounts from other banks reported on ChexSystems, that makes you ineligible to open a checking account anywhere. I think it would be a waste of time for both of us for you to fill out a loan application. Hell!" he continued with a chuckle, "I might even get written up, or even fired, for wasting the underwriter's time if I submitted this file to her. Have a good day, our business is done here!"

Cindy sank into a stupor, her skin feeling as if it was crawling with a painful static charge. Her vision of the banker blurred first, then the room all around him. Before she realized what was happening, she had lost all sense of where she was sitting. Her mind rolled back to her many issues, with each shred of depressing information piling on the last.

This was to be a great day of celebration. After years of living with her grandparents, William and Fran, due to the horrible incident between her and her step-father Randall that caused Cindy's mother to take his side and throw her out, she had finally landed a job that would allow her to move herself and her twin son and daughter into a luxury apartment of their own.

Sure, Cindy could have found a less expensive apartment than the one she chose, but she felt guilty for having her children share a bedroom in her grandparents' cramped house for so many years. Seeing the look of awe on her kids' faces when they went on play dates with their classmates to their big, beautiful houses was a constant reminder of the pain she felt growing up with her mother, the pain of not having anything, but having to sacrifice everything.

Cindy made a promise to herself that she would do whatever it took to not have her children experience the heartache and embarrassment of having to share clothes, or not being able to get the latest gadgets their friends had.

She had already plotted out her salary and discovered that it would be just enough to cover her increased living expenses, and also make the monthly payment on the defaulted student loans that she was recently able to work out a payment plan on to avoid having her wages garnished. Cindy had not made a payment on her student loans in more than two years. She had compiled massive loan debt over the seven years it took her to finish college.

She was what you would call a professional student. In fact, student loans were the only reason Cindy had any interest in going to college in the first place. She remembered feeling like she was wasting her time, sitting and listening to the loan coordinator explain the many benefits of using student loans and the importance of paying them back because her grandparents had cosigned for the loans, and they knew how it worked. All Cindy thought about in the meeting was how easy it was to get what she considered free money, and everything she could buy with it.

Through the years she used funds from her loans on everything from clothes, cars, and vacations, to renting plasma televisions for her and her children while throwing them large birthday parties.

Now she sat in the bank, after a failed attempt at opening up a checking account, which was the only requirement her new employer had, because the company only paid their employees through direct deposit. She was less concerned about not qualifying for a bank account, because all Cindy would do is just have the funds directly deposited into her grandparents' account that she used when she ran low on money.

However, what she could not shake was the embarrassing moment of staring at almost the lowest possible score attached to her name.

She coughed again, her breathing sputtering out for a moment before she collected herself and faced the stunned banker anew. The way he looked at her now was like she was the sum of something on the bottom of his shoe. Cindy tumbled into another fit of coughing. By the time she had finished, her skin felt clammy, her forehead was pouring sweat, and her eyes were watering.

"Are you okay?" Mr. Marks asked, looking away in disgust as he handed her a tissue. Cindy didn't bother with the tissue. She tried to gather as much pride as she could before she responded.

"I will be!"

"You said earlier that you take pride in helping people in my situation; so tell me how my credit score got so low."

With a slight roll of his eyes, Mr. Marks turned the screen back towards him and very rudely replied,

"You would receive that personal service if I was your personal banker; however, you are not the type of customer I or the bank want to add to our book of business, because of the risk. I compare helping people like you to a man giving birth to a child! Impossible. I do not mean to be rude, but my experience in dealing with your type has shown that you are stubborn in your ways, not disciplined in your finances, and quick to blame others for the problems you created for yourself. I cannot begin to tell you how much of my commissions I've had to pay back over the years because of irresponsible people like you overdrawing your bank accounts or defaulting on a your loans. So again, have a nice day!"

"Why you snake oil salesman!" Cindy yelled. "When you thought you could make money off of me, I was part of your mission."

"Now you find out I have some issues with my credit, and I've become your worst nightmare!"

"You were not sincere in your comments about helping the people!"

"You are only interested in helping yourself and the bank's bottom line!"

"It's professionals like you, and I use that term loosely, that give your profession a bad name!"

After her tirade, Cindy got up and stormed out of his office, slamming the door so hard behind her that the blinds fell off. As she started to leave the bank, with every step she took the walls began to narrow, and it seemed as if she was further and further away from the door.

She heard an eruption of laughter as she continued her journey to the exit.

Are those people laughing at me? she asked herself.

Was I that loud, that they heard everything I said?

After what seemed like an eternity, Cindy finally reached the door. Her mind raced as she walked out of the bank.

"Who can I call to get to the bottom of this?"

Cindy got in her car and slammed the door. She threw her purse against the passenger side window, catching her cell phone as it fell to the floor. Her heart raced as she scrolled through the contact list in her phone. Cindy's cough escalated as she reached the very last name in her contacts, becoming more distraught as she realized that the only person she could possibly ask for help in figuring out what happened to her credit was the person she trusted the least with her personal information; her older brother, Andrew.

"No way I am calling Andrew!" she said loudly to herself as she sped off.

"He's a lousy, good for nothing, blood-sucking scam artist, who is supposed to be this big time entrepreneur, but still finds a way to get money out of Grandma and Grandpa when he can't pay his bills."

"All he will probably do is swipe my social security number and attempt to get credit in my name. Shit, he might be the one who caused my credit to be ruined!" she mumbled.

As she drove through the intersection, it hit her that even if he tried to do something without her knowledge or consent, nothing would happen. From what the banker said at the bank, her credit score is the lowest he had ever seen, which means she had no options.

Whew, glad Grandma and the owner of the new apartment we're moving into are close friends from church! she thought to herself.

Because if not, she probably would have looked at my credit too. Dodged that bullet! she thought, with a relieved look on her face.

Cindy pulled into the parking lot of the rent-to-own store with a few minutes to spare.

I will call Andrew once I'm done here, she thought to herself as she entered the building.

**"The sacrifices we make to give our children the life
we didn't have, makes the struggle worth it in the end
when you see the smiles it puts on their faces." –Cindy**

"May I help you, ma'am?" a teenaged voice asked from behind the counter.

"Yes!" Cindy responded. "I have a two o'clock appointment with one of your rental agents, but I have to apologize, I seem to have forgotten his name."

"No problem, ma'am! I think I know who you are here to meet," replied the teenager. "Let me start with the easiest question you will be asked here today; what is your name?"

Normally she would have responded with a strong and confident voice, but after being mentally broken down from her visit at the bank she replied very meekly,

"My name is Cindy Johnson."

After typing in a few commands on the computer keyboard, the young teenager announced,

"Just as I thought."

Then he extended his hand and said,

"Hello, Ms. Johnson, my name is Marcus, and I will be your rental agent today. What brings you into our store?"

After two grueling hours, that seemed like two days for Cindy, of walking through the store being persuaded to upgrade on everything she'd selected to furnish her new apartment, Cindy found herself in a tough predicament. Would she use common sense and stick to the budget that she set for herself, that already had her maxed out financially? Or would she succumb to immediate gratification and an overzealous salesman?

"So what you are saying is it's only a hundred more per month for the full living room package?" Cindy confirmed as she sat on the plush leather sofa that crowned the living room display.

Marcus, an eager and gaunt young man, nodded vigorously as he responded.

"I don't look at it as an extra hundred dollars more a month. It's twenty-five dollars more a week. And who can't afford an extra twenty-five dollars for something they really want?"

Cindy smiled and shrugged. Certainly a woman with a new job, doing the best to claw toward the life her children deserve, can afford such a minor expense, she thought.

I'll just work some overtime plus, I have the child support payments I'm receiving for the kids to help with the added expense, she rationalized to herself.

"Okay, let's do it!"

After Cindy signed the contract and confirmed the delivery date, Marcus walked her to the door.

"This is very nice of you, Marcus."

"I really appreciate it!"

"No problem, Ms. Johnson; it's the least I can do for my favorite customer!"

"Aw!" she responded.

"You must say that to all your customers," she added, before erupting into a long sequence of coughing.

"No!" he answered, after she stopped.

"You are actually my very first customer ever, and I'm sure you made me rental agent of the month on my very first day on the job!"

"Whenever you are ready to upgrade your furniture package please let me know, I am here for all of your rental needs."

"And if you have any family or friends that you know who may need my services, please tell them about me!"

"You should get that cough checked out!"

"Yeah, I will," she responded.

"See you next time," he said, as she walked out the door.

Before driving off, she took a deep breath and replayed in her mind what had just happened in the store, and how she got to the point that she was not sure how much over her budget she actually went.

Cindy then picked up her phone and logged into Facebook to update her status.

"Wow, the sacrifices we make to give our children the life we didn't have, makes the struggle worth it in the end when you see the smiles it puts on their faces!"

I'll just make some minor adjustments tomorrow when I fill out my paperwork with human resources; we will be okay! she thought as she drove away.

"What do you mean I'm not able to turn the lights on in my apartment?" –Cindy

"What do you mean I'm not able to turn the lights on in my apartment?" Cindy shouted to the customer service rep sitting on the other side of the window.

"Sorry, Ms. Johnson, but our system shows that you have an outstanding balance of one thousand seven hundred and eighty-five dollars that was sent to collections a few years ago. So in order to receive new service in your name, you have to pay the balance in full, along with a thousand-dollar deposit!"

"What?! A thousand dollar deposit; are you kidding me?!?" Cindy screamed.

"Ma'am, ma'am, I want to help you sort this out, but you cannot keep talking to me this way."

After taking a few deep breaths, Cindy was able to compose herself enough to say before she started coughing,

"I apologize. I'm new at this, and figured the process of turning lights on in my new apartment would be much easier than this!"

"Excuse my coughing," Cindy asked.

"I think it comes about when I get in stressful situations!"

Empathizing with her, the rep responded,

"This is a stressful situation, with you scheduled to move in the day after tomorrow, so let's see if we can get to the bottom of this."

The rep and Cindy worked on confirming the information in the system and worked on a resolution for over an hour as the line behind her grew longer and longer, causing the shift supervisor to come over and investigate the problem.

After a few minutes, the supervisor announced rudely,

"Ms. Johnson, our hands are tied! Based on the information you provided my employee, I've come to the conclusion that she is correct in her findings!"

"You were provided the options you have to rectify the situation, so when you are ready, feel free to come back and I will take care of you personally; but until then I have to ask you to step aside so we can help the next person. Have a nice day."

"Wow, she got you, too." –Andrew

The next day, Cindy stood on the porch and aggressively knocked on the front door.

"Who is it?" the voice questioned as the door opened.

"Hello, Andrew. I have a problem!"

"Ha, I knew it!" Andrew responded.

"Knew what?" Cindy asked, in an agitated tone.

"Is that why you haven't returned any of my phone calls?"

"Yeah," Andrew responded.

"I figured you needed some money or something crazy like that!"

"Whatever!" she yelled in disgust.

"What gave you that idea? You know you are the last person I would call if I needed any money!"

"Your postings on Facebook!"

"My what?"

"Your Facebook postings!" he repeated.

"What the hell does the information I post on Facebook have to do with anything?"

With a sly laugh, Andrew responded with a long rant.

"From my experience, when a person expresses how great they feel, how in love they are or how successful they've become, it's usually the opposite. You have people changing their names to something like MonicaIDONTNEEDNOBODYCampbell, but always asking for a hand out, or JamesIWOULDNTCHANGEATHANGClarke, but wish they could turn back the hands of time to undo mistakes they made in the past. They always say don't judge a book by its cover; well, face it, little sis, Facebook is the new cover."

"So when I read your updates, I figured something was wrong, and eventually I would hear from you. So what's up?"

After taking a deep breath, Cindy responded.

"I'm not sure exactly the cause, but the effect is that my credit is jacked up!"

"When you use the term 'jacked up' to describe your credit, that means it must be really bad!" he confirmed.

"Let's just say that my credit is so bad that I could not even open up a free checking account, or have the power turned on in my new apartment!" Cindy expressed.

"Damn!" Andrew responded, before asking,

"Why don't you just call our dear rich brother to help you out? After all, you are his favorite between us two!" Andrew suggested sarcastically.

"I don't need anyone to rescue me; I just want answers. Besides, I haven't spoken with Bobby in quite some time now."

"It seems no one has!" Andrew replied.

"It's one thing for him to turn his back on us, but to disown Grandma and Grandpa the way he has after all they did for him, is just sad!"

"What does Jacob think about your situation?"

"He doesn't know," Cindy responded.

"How are you two doing these days? I was talking to Grams a few weeks ago, and she said she does not like the way he has been treating you lately."

"Grandma is just upset that Jacob is white. She needs to get over it, because things are a lot different now than they were forty years ago. Besides, I am not here to discuss my love life; that's none of your damn business!"

"Whoa, whoa; Jacob's race has nothing to do with anything!" Andrew responded.

"I know we did not have the best brother and sister relationship growing up, but I still love you. And I will not be ashamed or scared to tell you that I don't like or trust your boyfriend!"

"I love you too, and appreciate your concern. But you don't know Jacob, so you really can't make that assessment. So with this situation, let's just agree to disagree and get back to the reason why I'm here."

"Fair enough!"

Andrew responded before asking,

"Do you have a copy of your credit report so I can research the issue?"

"No, the guy at the bank told me it was against company policy to let me walk out with my report, but that I could request a free copy of my report when I receive the denial letter from the bank."

"Wow, sounds like that will take some time!"

"Time I don't have!" she emphasized, while struggling to hold back from coughing.

"You're in luck!" he announced.

"I just started a credit repair company, and the software that the startup kit comes with instantly allows me access to your credit report. All I need from you is a signature giving me your authorization, along with $285," he added.

"What, are you serious!? Two hundred and eighty-five dollars? Surely you jest!"

"No, I'm serious!"

"Why do I feel like I'm being taken advantage of by my brother, because of the desperate situation I'm in?"

"I'm not trying to take advantage of you. Believe me, I would do it for free, but I have to pay the vender for every credit report I pull, and after paying the money I had to pay to start this company, I just can't afford to pay for it out of my own pocket right now."

Feeling sick, Cindy started to cough and asked, "Can I use your bathroom?"

"Of course you can!" Andrew responded.

After a few minutes, Cindy returned with tears in her eyes. "Okay, let's do it."

Cindy gave Andrew all the information he needed, and after pulling her credit, it took her brother no time at all to figure out what happened.

Andrew took a deep breath before shaking his head as he looked up at his little sister and said, "Wow, she got you too!"

"I'm never going to make the same mistakes you made!" –Cindy

"Eight lines of credit and utilities all sent to collections or charged off, Mother!" Cindy barked into her cell phone.

"Eight?!" she questioned in disbelief.

By now her mother, Melanie, had run out of things to say in her defense. There was a mumbling from the other end of the line that sounded either like crying or laughing. Cindy couldn't tell which.

"How could you take eight lines of credit out in my name and let them all go to collections?"

"What kind of mother ruins their children's childhood and jeopardizes their future with the selfish decisions she made, and then continues on with her happy life with that pedophile with no care whatsoever of the negative impact it's causing on her children?" Cindy asked.

"He's not a pedophile!" Melanie angrily replied.

Cindy roared off the highway, coming to park on the shoulder. She was too angry to continue driving.

"You're still defending him...?" Her statement is interrupted by another violent fit of coughing. By the time she was finished, it was clear that her mother was crying. "You really do care more about him than your own children?" she asked.

There was a long moment of soft sobbing before Melanie finally spoke.

"I'm sorry," she sighed before continuing. "I didn't want to be alone."

"If I could go back and do it all over again, I would right my wrongs; but I was desperate when your father got locked up, and had no other options! As a parent yourself, you will soon find out first-hand of the tough decisions you must make daily! I can only hope you take a different path from the one I went down," she continued, before being interrupted.

"I will take a different path because I am nothing like you, Mother! I haven't, and never will, throw my kids under the bus to keep a sorry excuse for a man from leaving me! I may not have been able to stop you from ruining my credit, but I can damn sure guarantee that neither you, nor this situation, will get in the way of the life I'm building for me and my children. I'm never going to make the same mistakes you made!"

"But, Cindy," Melanie called...

"Good bye, Mother. I never want to see you again!" Cindy yelled, before throwing down the phone.

"Financial hardship is not just a black issue Chica; it's also a major problem in the Latino community too." –Larissa

"Larissa!"

"Yes, Mami?" Larissa responded, before being surprised as she entered the living room.

"Oh my God, Cindy!" she yelled, as she rushed over to give her a big hug.

"Hey, Larissa, how are you?"

"I'll leave you two alone so you can catch up. It was good seeing you, Cindy!" Larissa's mother expressed.

"Good seeing you as well, Ms. Mariano."

"Ok, what's wrong, Cindy?" Larissa asked so quickly, her mother had not even exited the living room completely.

"It always amazes me how you can tell when something is bothering me," Cindy responded.

"Your face and low energy says it all," Larissa added.

As tears started to flow, Cindy cried out, "It's bad, and I didn't know who else I could go to."

"What's wrong?" Larissa asked, as she grabbed Cindy's hand and led her to the front porch to talk.

"It's my family," Cindy announced.

"What about your family? Is everything okay?"

"I've always envied your family because you always exuded love and respect towards each other and you were financially stable, while my family was the stereotypical dysfunctional, broke black family on the block!"

Confused, Larissa asked, "Why do you say that?"

She listened intently as her distraught friend talked about the inferiority complex she developed over the years due to the shame and embarrassment of her family's financial struggle. Cindy outlined in detail the pain she experienced in the past, and the hardships she will face in the future.

"Wow! Larissa responded after Cindy finished.

"I see why we are such great friends; we share the same story."

Puzzled by what Larissa just stated, Cindy asked,

"What do you mean?"

"While you were busy being envious of me, I was dreaming of switching places with you!"

"What? I don't understand," Cindy responded.

"Financial hardship is not just a black issue Chica; it's also a major problem in the Latino community too".

Larissa took a deep breath and looked Cindy in the eye and continued, "There are eight of us who live here in this two-bedroom apartment, because we have no other options."

"But I thought you all decided to stay and help your mother after her horrible diagnosis," Cindy responded.

"No, not at all. Our sad reality is that none of us can get our own places because we all have bad credit. Shit, I just lost a job offer I received because when they did a pre-employment background check on me, it was discovered that I had three cars repossessed, among other things."

"You had what?"

"You heard me right, three!"

"All before I turned 16!" Larissa disclosed.

Shocked, Cindy asked, "How the hell did that happen?"

"My mother ruined our credit the same way your mother ruined yours. And now she is sick, and has no medical insurance to help cover her medical bills. So it's a win-win; she allows us to stay here with her, and we help her pay her bills. But what's sad is the fact that my sister has acted out of desperation, and has justified opening a credit card in my niece's name, starting a whole new cycle of hardship."

Larissa continued talking for over an hour, as she detailed the hardships her and her family face daily as they struggle to get by before ending by saying, "Our lives are screwed up because my mother sacrificed our futures to take care of her present. You are fortunate to have grandparents like you do who will help you in a time of need. So if they are allowing you to use the money in their account to pay off your bills, do it. I could only wish that I had grandparents like yours."

As they both sat on the porch with tears in their eyes, Cindy smiled and said, as she reached to give her friend a hug, "I love you, Larissa!"

"I love you too, Cindy!"

"I've dropped the ball!" –Cindy

"Okay, great, so everything is set and transferred to my name?" Cindy asked the agent over the phone.

"Yes, Ms. Johnson. The account is showing a zero balance, and by tomorrow morning the system will update with you being the account holder."

"Perfect!"

"Is there anything else I can help you with today, Ms. Johnson?"

"No, that's it; have a great day!" she responded before hanging up the phone.

"Thank you, God!" Cindy said in a soft whisper as she closed her eyes. She was able to get the power turned on in her new apartment by both paying off the past due amount and the thousand-dollar deposit, using the account her grandparents gave her access to.

Cindy did not ask for their approval, figuring she would replenish the money before they knew it was gone. Suddenly there was a loud scream coming from her son's room. Cindy turned and ran down the hall to investigate the matter.

"What's wrong, baby?" she asked.

"I hate this place!" her son answered angrily. "I want to go back to Grandma's. I miss my friends already!"

Cindy, knowing the real reason for the blow up, looked down at her baby boy, who looked up at her tearfully. She said,

"I'm sorry, honey. I did not think to get a PlayStation for you."

"PlayStation *Three*," her son corrected. "Everyone has one but me," he continued. Hearing her son express his sadness immediately caused Cindy to become flushed with guilt. She could relate to his disappointment, because that's all she experienced growing up. She had made it her life's mission to do whatever it took to ensure that her children did not go through what she went through as a child. The pain of feeling less than, by not measuring up to their friends.

I've dropped the ball! Cindy thought to herself.

Cindy stepped to the side, pulling her son along with her to get out of the way of the movers carrying in the boxes. With the furniture people delivering all the furniture, including the flat-screen televisions, at the same time, it was major chaos in her new apartment.

Cindy beat back a sudden cough and pulled her son into an embrace. "It's okay, sweetie. I know exactly how you feel. I moved away from all of my friends when I was around your age too, and I must say, I think I turned out just fine!" she replied with a soft smile.

"Give it some time, and you will see how great this move will be for all three of us! And who knows; maybe after a couple months of paying on the furniture, they will allow me to add the PlayStation Three to the account," Cindy said warmly to her increasingly frustrated son.

"What if I take us out to dinner after we finish unpacking to celebrate?" she asked.

The boy pulled away with a frown on his face.

"We could go to Chuck E. Cheese," Cindy offered with a grin. "But we have to hurry, because Jacob is coming by later."

Her son did his best to hide his smile with a renewed effort at scowling, but in time, he couldn't help himself. He beamed and skipped excitedly down the hall, then he hollered the good news to his sister:

"Put some shoes on, big head; Mom's taking us to Chuck E. Cheese!"

"That's crazy; you don't budget based off of assumptions!" –Jacob

Cindy stood nervously as Jacob, her boyfriend, took a walk around her new apartment.

"Not bad," He announced as he turned the corner of the hallway, heading back towards her.

"How much are the rent and utilities a month?"

Nervously, Cindy responded,

"Well, the rent is eleven eighty."

"Eleven what?" Jacob interrupted.

"Did you fall on your head or something?"

"How are you going to afford that a month with the salary you will make?"

Expecting this response from him, Cindy already had an answer prepared.

"I will work as much overtime as possible."

"That's crazy; you don't budget based on assumptions, Cindy. There is no guarantee that working overtime would be an option!"

"Well, I can also use the child support that I'm receiving for the kids—"

"Hell no! You are tripping now! You promised me that you would give me that money every month. That's why I bought my new motorcycle!"

"I told you when you first started talking that silly shit about getting your own apartment that it was a stupid idea and you should just move in with me. But you didn't want to listen to me. Now look at what you've done!"

"Break the lease and move in with me!"

"But I can't."

"What do you mean you can't?"

"I'm sure there's a penalty, and plus the landlord is a good friend of my grandmother's."

"Do I look like I care about who she is?"

"You need around-the-clock help managing your money, so check this out," Jacob stated, as he walked to the door. "You have three days to fix this shit, or we are done!"

"But Jacob—" Cindy called out as he slammed the door behind him

"How?"

She turned with tears in her eyes as she navigated around the many boxes stacked in the hallway, and headed to the kitchen to make herself a cup of coffee.

After a couple of hours of rationalizing, Cindy finally came to her senses.

He's right!

She thought to herself.

"I can understand why he is so upset with me. I should've moved in with him like he suggested in the first place."

Jacob has sacrificed so much for me and the kids over the last six months, which is more than I can say about their own father, who wants nothing to do with them. It's amazing that he even pays child support for them, she continued to think.

"The least I can do for Jacob to show my appreciation is to give him the support payments like I promised him so he can pay for his bike. He is a good man, and I don't want to lose him!"

Cindy raced to the bedroom to retrieve her cell phone to call Jacob. After a couple of failed attempts at getting him to answer, she decided to log into Facebook and tag Jacob as she gave a status update. "My knight in shining armor has shown up at my new doorsteps and rescued me from myself once again. YES I will move in with you, because I would be lost without you!"

"There; he'll get that, and everything will be fine! I love that man!" She thought with a smile as she logged off, *I really do!*

"Am I just like my mother?" –Cindy

"Cindy, how could you?"

Not feeling well, and caught off guard at the line of questioning from her grandmother, Cindy just stood silently.

"How could you?" Fran asked again.

"What do you mean? How could I what?" she finally answered, with a puzzled look on her face.

"How could you abuse our generosity and trust we had in you?"

"What are you talking about? You gave me access to your account in case of emergency, and I had one. Plus, I'm replenishing the money in a few weeks, so I don't see what the big deal is!"

Agitated and saddened by Cindy's unapologetic stance, Fran became emotional as she yelled,

"First of all, I find out you moved like a thief in the night from the apartment you just moved into, giving no notice or explanation to anyone. All to shack up with some guy you just met, with no concern of how it could impact the kids. Showing no appreciation for the strings you asked me to pull for you, potentially jeopardizing a friendship I've had for over forty years.

"Then, if that wasn't enough heartbreak and disappointment, I go to the bank to withdraw some money from the emergency account that your grandfather and I set up and had never used, only to find out that it's overdrawn by more than three thousand dollars!

"When the teller gave me the shocking news I just knew it was a mistake. So when I questioned her about the situation, she called the service banker over to assist me. The service banker ended up printing out transactions that I was unaware of that went back more than three years. The last transaction was a debit for almost three thousand dollars from the utility company, which took place last week, that overdrew the account!"

Stopping herself before she continued, Fran stated,

"Why am I going into detail about everything, because you already know? So again, Cindy, how could you?"

Upset at the tone her grandmother spoke to her in,

Cindy responded,

"If you didn't want me to use the account, then you should not have given me access to it!"

"Oh, I see! You want to blame your selfish decision to overdraw our account on us! The only thing your grandfather and I are guilty of is being so concerned about you and the kids' security and well-being, that we lost focus on ours!"

Fran started sobbing uncontrollably as she walked to the door. Before she exited the apartment, she turned to look at her granddaughter and mouthed the words that sent a dagger through Cindy's heart.

"As hard as we tried, you still turned out no different from your mother. We are cutting you off!"

Shaken from the words her grandmother spoke to her, Cindy ran to the bedroom and cried like she had never cried before. Could it be? Was her grandmother right? Had what she feared more than anything in life, come to pass?

Am I just like my mother? she wondered to herself. *Am I?*

"That crazy old woman doesn't know what she's talking about! Anyway, who needs family, when I have Jacob?"

"Spring cleaning is done and the trash is taken out!" –Cindy

Cindy stood coughing while staring out the window, watching as Jacob pulled into the driveway.

"Where's my bike?"

Jacob asked excitedly, as he stormed into the apartment.

Not mentally ready to deal with the confrontation, Cindy acted as if she didn't hear him.

"Cindy? Cindy!" Jacob called again.

"Yes?" she finally answered.

"Where the hell is my motorcycle?"

In a soft, nervous tone, she delivered the bad news.

"They came and picked it up."

In an elevated tone, Jacob questioned,

"Who came and picked it up?"

"The bank."

"The bank? Why?"

"Lack of payment."

"What do you mean, lack of payment? I thought the child support money was going straight to the finance company?"

"It was, but I told you that the children's father lost his job, so I have not received any money for the last few months." It was a lie, but Cindy did not know what else to say.

Cindy extended her hand to give him a beer, but Jacob swatted it away before pushing her so hard against the refrigerator that it knocked the dishes off the top of it, causing them to crash on top of her as she lay on the floor.

"It was a couple payments away from being paid off. It's your fault!" he screamed as he stood over her.

"You told me you were guaranteed overtime hours now that you have some seniority, so you lied to me about that, too. Are you cheating on me or something?"

"No! I've been working overti–!" Cindy tried to answer before being cut off.

"Shut up, bitch, before I kick you in the head. You and your snotty-nosed kids have been nothing but an albatross around my neck since I met you. I'm moving out!" Jacob announced, as he stormed out the door.

Cindy struggled to gather herself as she unsuccessfully wiped the tears away from her eyes. She soon became overwhelmed with the pain of having to accept the fact that her brother Andrew was correct in his assessment of Jacob.

The mental and physical abuse started shortly after moving in with him, but Cindy figured he was just stressed out after being forced to downsize and move into a two-bedroom apartment when he lost his home to foreclosure, and had to file for bankruptcy from years of bad financial decisions. After time, she figured it would get better; but it didn't. Already maxed out financially, Cindy found herself struggling even more to stay afloat because she had to support Jacob, who was unemployed, but refused the two job offers he received because he felt the positions were beneath him. But he still wanted the best of everything, and Cindy obliged him.

To show his appreciation for Cindy using the child support payments she received from the children's father to pay for his motorcycle, Jacob used his bike as a way to impress other women. Cindy initially caught wind of his exploits from pictures she saw in his phone that popped up on the iCloud, but decided to turn the other cheek because in her mind, a bad man was better than no man at all, especially when the alternative would be raising the kids as a single parent.

The straw that broke the camel's back was when one of the women that the love of her life cheated on her with showed up at her job, pregnant with what she said was Jacob's baby.

"I have to be strong. I cannot let anyone in the family know that Jacob and I are no longer together!" she thought, as she started to clean up the broken dishes.

Shortly after she finished, Cindy reached for her cell phone and logged into Facebook and posted for the world to see:

"Spring cleaning is done, and the trash is taken out. Man, I love my new life!"

"Ma, what's the credit card number again?"

A couple of months later, the phone in Cindy's office rang. She answered, "Hello."

"Ma, what's the credit card number again?" the voice asked over the phone. It was Ariel, Cindy's daughter, doing what had become a ritual every night; ordering takeout.

Because of the financial hole she'd dug for herself, Cindy had no choice but to work a second job in a futile attempt to break even. Sure, she could not afford it, and both of her kids were chubbier than their peers due to the unhealthy lifestyle, but she felt guilty working so many hours and being away from her children all the time. She justified spending more than two hundred dollars a month on fast food because that made them happy, and gave her peace of mind, knowing she was putting a smile on their faces every night.

"Again, Ariel? I thought I told you to write it down," Cindy responded, as she pulled the card from her wallet.

Because Fran and William had cut Cindy off financially and cancelled her access to their bank account a while back, she'd had no choice but to open an account up in her daughter's name so her job could deposit her money. She also somehow found a way to open a credit card in Ariel's name, as well pledging not to abuse it, like her mother did.

"Okay, young lady, one more time. I have a lot of work to do," Cindy disclosed, before giving her daughter the card number.

"Thanks, Mom, love you!"

"Love you too!"

**"I stressed the importance of being prepared
for any type of emergency, especially with
you having young children." –Stanley**

Cindy knocked on her boss' opened door. Stanley is his name, and even though he was very demanding to work for, she knew he genuinely cared about his staff. He smiled when he saw her. She wished she could return the smile, but at this moment, Cindy was feeling entirely too confused. In her hand, she held an opened envelope, containing a bill from the clinic she'd recently visited to inquire about the persistent cough she had ignored, but had plagued her for the past couple of years. She had provided the doctor with all of her employment information so he could run the test and now she stood there, with an astronomical amount she had to pay back.

"Something I can help you with, Cindy?" Stanley asked in the fatherly way she always adored.

She showed him the bill. "I'm confused as to why I received this; shouldn't our insurance plan cover it?" In truth, she was more agitated than she was letting on. The reality of having to pay one thousand eight hundred and forty-five dollars for the battery of tests, despite paying into the company health insurance plan every month, had her justifiably steamed.

At first Stanley looked startled, then saddened by the question. His face turned white as he took a moment to gather himself. "You don't remember then?" he asked her.

"Remember what?" she inquired, with her voice catching in her throat.

"You opted out of the health insurance plan when you filled out your new hire paperwork when you first started with us. When I noticed you declined any type of coverage, I stressed the importance of being prepared for any type of emergency, especially with you having young children. Here, let me get your paperwork so I can show you."

As Stanley stood to retrieve her employment papers, Cindy relived the very moment she made the awful decision to deny any type of insurance, potentially exposing her family to every type of risk imaginable.

No way! Cindy thought to herself, as she remembered the moment. It was the day after she blew through her budget while renting furniture for her apartment. In order to afford everything she'd selected, Cindy had to trim the fat from her paycheck by not paying for something she did not value. Even though she felt it was time for her to be more responsible with her finances, since she was moving out of her grandparents' house, her immediate need for gratification, along with the advice her grandfather always preached about paying for insurance or into a retirement plan being a huge waste of money, made the decision easy. She even declined participating in the 401K plan offered at work, and used the extra cash for something she found value in.

"Here it is, Cindy, where you declined coverage."

As Stanley pointed to her signature opting out of the plan, Cindy said,

"That's okay, I remember."

"I do have one last question though," she added.

"Sure, Cindy, what is it?"

With a puzzled look on her face she asked "If money is not being taken out of my check for insurance, what is it being taken out for?"

Stanley turned and answered in a sympathetic tone, "The IRS!"

"What do you mean, the IRS?"

"The payroll department received a letter from them demanding us to send one hundred and eighty-five dollars a month out of your check. We don't ask any questions because by law, we have no choice but to comply with their request. You didn't receive notification from either the IRS or payroll making you aware of the situation?"

"I'm not sure; I don't open my mail if I don't know what it is."

"Why do you think they would be garnishing my wages?"

"I'm not sure, but if you want, we can look at your paperwork to see if something stands out."

"Sure, what do I have to lose?" responded Cindy.

After a few tense minutes of watching her boss scan over her paperwork, he announced,

"Here it is."

"You filed EXEMPT status, which means the IRS takes little to nothing from your check."

"I would correct this immediately if I were you; it will only get worse!"

The IRS is already garnishing my wages, making my check less than it should be; when I change my status from EXEMPT it will make my check even smaller! Cindy thought to herself.

"Thanks for your help, Stanley." Cindy replied, as she got up to walk out of his office.

"Not a problem at all, Cindy. Good luck with everything and please, take care of that exempt status," he urged, as she disappeared down the hall.

For the first time in her life, she had no clue what to do. She had no one to lean on, no one to call for support. Cindy was all alone. Overwhelmed by her extremely dire circumstances, Cindy retreated to the ladies room. As she wiped the tears from her eyes, Cindy stared at her reflection in the mirror. *Wow!* she thought, *What have I done to myself?* Cindy was forced for the first time to stop and look at the irreversible damage her bad financial practices had caused her.

She struggled as she tried to recognize the image being reflected back to her. An image of a face that looked ten years older than it actually was, from the dark, puffy circles around her once brightly lit eyes, to her hair that looked like it hadn't been tended to in months.

After letting out a series of coughs, Cindy wiped her face and said to herself as she walked out of the bathroom,

I'm a wreck!

"Here are the terms of your new agreement, Ms. Johnson; by now you are a pro at this."
–Lending agent

"Okay, Cindy, get well soon," the voice said on the other end of the phone before hanging up. Cindy had called in sick for the third day in a row. In fact, over the last two months she has missed more than five weeks of work, burning through all of her sick days after being instructed by her doctor to take time off from work. Even though it meant she would have little to no income coming in, she seemed at peace with the idea of spending more time with her children.

As she put her cell phone down a voice said:

"Here are the terms of your new agreement, Ms. Johnson; by now you are a pro at this!" The lending agent smiled as she spoke.

Because Cindy has no short-term disability or any other type of insurance to cover the money she lost from her missed days of work, she was forced to use various payday loan services throughout the city to help bridge the gap. As soon as she paid the money back, along with all the interest and fees, Cindy would take out another loan right on the spot.

As she grabbed a pen to sign the new agreement, she yelled in disbelief:

"Twenty-three percent interest! I thought after the fifth time of using your services I automatically received a break in the rate I must pay back? At this rate, I'm paying back almost double the amount I'm borrowing!"

"Normally that is the case; but since you were late with your last payment, the system has flagged you as a risky customer, and therefore you are required to pay a higher rate. If you need time to think about it, we will be here until 5:30."

"No, I'll take the money," Cindy agreed somberly.

"Can I use your pen? This one doesn't work."

"What's wrong, baby?" –Fran

A few months went by, and now Cindy was huddled beside her bed, clutching her cell phone against her cheek, as she listened to the ring crank through. When her grandmother answered, she immediately began to sob.

"Cindy?" Fran asked, clearly happy to hear her voice. "Is that you?"

Cindy nodded as she sniffed. "Yeah, Grandma, it's me."

"How have you been, dear? Your grandfather and I have missed you and the children so much."

Through the tears, all Cindy could muster was a mumbled, "I've missed you, too!"

Hearing the distress in her granddaughter's response, Fran asked, "What's wrong, baby?"

Cindy shuddered as she drew a long, pained breath. "I need some help, Grandma!"

There was a long silence from the other end of the line. "What do you need? We...we don't have any money."

"Grandma!" Cindy yelled, as she broke into a deeper sob.

"Yes, dear?"

"I have cancer!"

Andrew

"Where did I go wrong?"
–Andrew

Andrew took a sip of water as he leaned back in his chair. He put his head in his hands in an attempt to relax his nerves after a long, grueling day of trying to justify the actions that brought him to this moment in time. "Where did I go wrong?" he asked himself.

After a few minutes, Andrew's mind started to wander, losing all control of the events being rehashed in his head. It was as if a Higher Power had taken over, forcing his mind to replay the series of bad financial decisions, one after the other, that not only ruined *his* life, but the lives of the many people who loved and trusted in him the most.

"Just fill out this credit card application,
and the T-shirt is yours."
–Emily

"Excuse me," the voice called, as Andrew walked out of the student center. When he turned to face the person talking to him, it was love at first sight. He went speechless looking at the most beautiful girl he had ever seen. "Would you like a free T-shirt?" the young lady asked sparking Andrew's interest as he thought to himself, *Hell yeah, along with your number!*

As he gained his composure he responded, "What do I need to do?"

"Just fill out this credit card application, and the T-shirt is yours."

"If I have to fill something out, then it's not really free, is it? I'm just saying."

Caught off guard from his uncanny response, the young lady had no reply, so she stood there and just smiled, before Andrew let her off the hook. Laughing, he stated, "I'm just playing with you. Where do I sign?"

As he completed the application Andrew asked, "So, what's your name?"

"Emily," she responded.

"You got a boyfriend?"

"No."

"Can I have your number?"

Intrigued by Andrew's charisma, it was easy for Emily to comply with his request and give him her number. After all he was tall, handsome, confident and funny, unlike most of the guys she'd met on campus thus far. As Andrew walked away with his T-shirt he turned and said, "I will call you tonight." Waving back at him Emily shook her head as she thought to herself, *Looking forward to it, Mr. Johnson.*

"Going through receipts, why?" –Andrew

A couple of months later, Andrew impatiently waited for Emily downstairs before finally deciding to go up to her dorm to see what was causing the delay. When she let him in, he felt his temperature start to rise at the sight of her still dressed in her gym clothes, which meant she had not even showered yet. As he turned away to hide his frustration, he couldn't help but notice the mounds of paper sprawled all over her bed. He asked, "What are you doing with all of that mess on your bed? Are you recycling or something?"

"I'm going through my receipts," she responded.

"Going through receipts, why? Looks like a pile of trash to me."

"You have buyer's remorse and looking for the receipt to return something?"

"No, not at all. My father has preached to me the importance of money management since I was in the fourth grade, and this is one of the many ways he's taught me to track my expenses."

Still upset about being late for the party, Andrew responded, "I think it's a waste of time! We are in college, right? So, we should be smart enough to mentally track where our money is going without collecting a bunch of trash like we're pack rats or something!"

As Emily started to respond, Andrew cut her off. "Let's just agree to disagree and end this, because it's time to get our groove on!!!"

**"You sure you want to miss the fella's faces
when I unveil my new investment to them?"
–Andrew**

A year later, as Andrew and Emily sat alone in the office with tension so thick you could slice it with a knife, Andrew said,

"Baby, everything will be fine, don't worry!"

"I don't understand how. Your summer job ends next week, and it's impossible with the demands of your class schedule to work during the school year. I don't think it's a wise decision! We've had extensive talks about our future together, and the one thing that can sabotage it is you not respecting the value of money!"

Always knowing how to smooth over a rough situation, Andrew said,

"I love you, baby!"

Emily tried to respond before being interrupted by the opening of the squeaky office door.

"Okay, Andrew, you're all set. Don't hesitate to call me with any questions. And please, if you have any family or friends in the market, let them know about the great service I provided to you today."

Waving at the car salesman as he pulled away from the dealership, Andrew was on cloud nine. "Feel the power in the engine, baby! There is nothing like the smell of a new car!" he continued in excitement.

Smells like cigarettes to me! Emily thought to herself in disbelief. Disbelief that, after she gave Andrew her opinion, he still allowed his immediate need for gratification to take precedence over their future together.

As sadness started to take over she said, "Let me out at the plaza. I will hook up with you later."

"You sure you want to miss the fella's faces when I unveil my new investment to them?"

"I'm sure it will be a great day in history but I'll pass, because I have a few supplies I need for class next week."

"Besides, I wouldn't brag about investing in a depreciating asset!"

"Whatever," he responded, as he pulled up to the entrance of the plaza.

As Emily exited the car, Andrew looked at her adoringly and said, "Happy anniversary, baby girl!"

Hiding her disappointment, she waved and smiled back and responded, "Back at you!"

**"I will never stress about money. I'm young and
have the rest of my life to make more."
–Andrew**

A few weeks later, Andrew walked into his dorm room with his arms full of bags from McDonald's. "I'm back; hope you're hungry!" When he didn't hear Emily respond, he went into his bedroom to see if she was still there. As he entered the room, he found her sitting on his bed, reading a piece of paper. "Baby, did you hear me? I got some Mickey Ds so we can celebrate."

When she turned toward Andrew, she had the look of disappointment written all over her face. "What is this?" she asked, as she handed him the paper she was holding.

"Nothing really," he answered, after looking at the document.

"What do you mean, nothing? I can read. It's a collection letter from the credit card company demanding payment on your delinquent account."

"You lied to me. You told me you took care of this!"

"It's no big deal," he responded. "I will call them and pay the whole balance off with my next student loan disbursement."

"Are you kidding me? That's over two months away! You can't go that long without communicating with them! Who knows, you might even be able to work something out in your favor; but to go so long without talking with them is not wise! Plus, you said you paid everything off with your *last* disbursement, and you obviously didn't."

"Baby, the food is getting cold. I promise to take care of this immediately. Now let's go eat."

Emily took a deep breath and hugged him, then she looked Andrew in the eyes and said "You've already had to drop two classes this semester to take on a part-time job, delaying your graduation, all to pay on a car you could've waited to get when you finished college. How you handle this situation will not only affect the rest of your life, but potentially our future as well, so please take this seriously!"

"I will, I promise!"

She smiled and took another breath, then asked, "What are we celebrating?"

As they both turned towards the kitchen he answered,

"I got a new sound system and chrome rims for the car."

"You did what?" she responded in disappointment.

"How did you pay for them?"

With a puzzled look on his face, he answered, "My credit card, of course!"

"You mean to tell me you used the remaining available balance on your credit card to trick out that clunker? All in an effort to impress a bunch of guys on campus who aren't really your friends?" she stated, while shaking her head.

"Andrew, you just made me lose my appetite. I'm leaving!"

"Baa-" Andrew called, before being cut off.

"As much as I loved the idea of having a future with you, I must end it."

"What?" Andrew asked. "Why?"

"*You* are that irresponsible guy my father warned me about! You are so focused on impressing people that you've lost sight of what's most important!"

Upset at what she'd just told him, Andrew responded, "I'm so tired of you trying to control me! I'm totally capable of making grown-man decisions. Plus, your father doesn't even know me!"

With a cracked voice Emily responded, "I've suffered enough in silence and turned the other cheek with every bad decision you've made with your money, so as much as it pains me, I have to do what's best for me and my future… I love you, and hope you get your life together!"

Andrew responds, "Get my life together? I hope you get *yours* together! All I ever hear is 'my daddy showed me this' or 'my daddy taught me that'. No, what your daddy's done is made you into a boring, too-serious-about-life little daddy's girl! I will never stress about money. I'm young and have the rest of my life to make more. Plus, if I need some quick cash, all I have to do is call my grandparents, who, unlike your daddy, will not lecture me or ask any questions."

"That's your problem now!" Emily responded.

"No!" Andrew continued. "Your problem is you can't see what's in front of your face! You can tell from all the heads that turn when I'm cruising around campus that there are many other chicks vying for your spot as my lady, a spot you obviously do not appreciate having! So go ahead and leave, and when you call your daddy tonight, make sure you tell him thanks for doing us both a favor!"

Emily ran to retrieve her belongings from his room, and as she was leaving, she looked at him with tears in her eyes, then turned and walked out of Andrew's life forever.

Wow! he thought to himself as he came to. *I thought she was trying to control me. How different would my life have been if I only listened to her?*

Deeply saddened at this point, he sat up to take a deep breath, then hunched back over when suddenly there was a sneeze. He was so focused in his thoughts, he was startled. Instinctively, he looked in the direction of the noise and noticed an older lady staring back at him, shaking her head. *Sister Hancock, what is she doing here?* he thought, as he rolled his eyes at her.

The sight of her unleashes another horrible memory that Andrew will never forget.

"I don't want to appear desperate." –Andrew

"Brother Johnson, you are a godsend!"

"I appreciate it, Pastor James. Let me know if there is anything else I can help you or the congregation with."

"Actually there is, Andrew."

"Sure, anything, Pastor; what is it?"

"I would love it if you would consider leading our newly formed finance ministry."

"It's an honor to be considered, and I would love to do it. But first I must make sure I'm not breaking any rules."

"Being a licensed financial advisor means that I'm held to the highest ethical standards and must follow them to a tee. So, can I let you know in a couple of days?"

"Take as long as you need, Brother Johnson. It would be a true blessing to the church having someone of your caliber lead our team!"

"God bless!"

"God bless you too, Pastor!"

As Andrew exited the sanctuary, he found it difficult to keep a straight face. *Keep your composure, Drew!* he thought to himself.

He walked through the parking lot, finally reaching his car. He turned as he sat down to see if anyone was outside. After realizing he was all alone he lost it and screamed:

"Woo! Hell yeah!"

His mother showed him the many ways to take advantage of the numerous churches they joined when he was growing up. They were a family of four with no father, so it was easy for his mother to tug at the hearts of the congregation when they needed help financially.

Andrew's mother would plant seeds by giving a small offering at one church Sunday morning, then that very afternoon watch earlier seeds she'd planted grow by standing and requesting help from another. She felt justified in her actions because really, how could a single mother of three young children afford to give the family's hard-earned money to help sustain a church and not expect anything in return?

In her mind, the churches were obligated to support the members and those in the community that needed help. It was the law of large numbers philosophy she followed, so the more churches they joined, the more help they could get.

Over the last three years, Andrew had lost count of how many churches he had joined in an effort to achieve what he had achieved today. His hard work had finally paid off. It did not matter if it was against company policy to join the finance committee; he would've done it anyway. He only made the comment because he wanted to appear totally ethical in his business dealings, knowing that if the newly appointed, young, and dynamic pastor fully trusted him, he would approve any suggestion he made.

He couldn't care less about adding value to the church and its parishioners. All Andrew was focusing on was increasing his personal income, and being hand-picked by Pastor James to lead the finance ministry would give him instant credibility and access to over 2,200 church members to solicit his products and services.

Even though I told him a couple of days, I will wait and call Pastor James next week and accept the position. I don't want to appear desperate! Andrew thought to himself, as he drove away with a smile on his face.

"All I need is one." –Andrew

Three months later, as Andrew was finishing lunch, he began to study the list of names for the first prospect he would solicit from the committee members he hand-picked for the team. Unbeknownst to Pastor James, Andrew focused less on selecting the best-qualified members for the finance ministry, but more on the person who would be the better match for his products and services.

He strategically did not include anyone who had any experience in finance or worked in the finance field. He wanted to avoid being challenged on his financial advice, and he also did not want to take the chance of having to compete with another advisor for the large amount of business he believed it would generate.

"This is going to be a goldmine!" Not only did he plan to solicit his insurance and investment services, but also the new credit repair service he was thinking about starting as well.

"All I need is one!" he thought, as he scanned the room. "That one would spread the word on how great I am, and the next thing you know, I'll not only have their friends and family, but also their coworkers running to me for help! They all would unknowingly become soldiers in my army."

Right as Andrew was finishing the thought, he was interrupted.

"Excuse me, Brother Johnson."

"Yes, Sister Davis; can I help you with something?"

"A few of us were discussing during the lunch break the fact that we don't understand why we have to allow you to pull our credit, and also look at our personal budgets."

Expecting this issue would arise, Andrew already had a response prepared, answering,

"That's a valid question, Sister Davis. But first let me start by stressing how much Pastor James and I appreciate you all volunteering to serve on the finance ministry. But let me ask you this; how can you truly help your brothers and sisters in Christ with their finances, if you are potentially struggling with the same issues yourselves?"

"Remember, none of you have a background in finance, so allowing me to pull your credit and look at your monthly budgets will ensure that you are not headed down the same dead end road as they are."

"Don't worry; the worst thing that could possibly happen is that we find that there is someone in here who needs my help in certain areas of their personal finances. I can assure you, that information will stay between us!"

Knowing that the most effective way to close a deal was to tug at a prospect's heart, Andrew ended his response by saying,

"So let go, and let God!"

After a brief moment of silence, a voice was heard whispering in the back of the room.

"Shoot, my mama ain't raise no fool. I'm going to take advantage of this free help!"

The room suddenly erupted in laughter as the committee members relaxed their concerns. One after the other they all not only gave Andrew their social security numbers and other information to pull their credit, but also scheduled individual appointments with him, too. Andrew's plan was taking shape faster than he ever imagined. He smiled as he thought about how he would spend all the money he would make off of the deals.

After finishing with signing everyone up for their appointments, Andrew closed by saying, "Thank you, everyone, for your input today, and your willingness to do God's work in not only helping your fellow members, but yourselves as well. I am very excited about the future of this committee, and the joy it will bring me to serve with you! I will see a few of you next week at your homes; the others, the week after. So go with God! Now let me close with a prayer."

"She's mine." –Andrew

"Hello, Mia, it's Andrew. How are you?"

"I'm great! Are you on your way?"

"Yes, I am; but unfortunately I am running a few minutes late. My last client meeting ran a few minutes over, so I understand if you want to cancel our meeting."

"No, that's fine!" Mia responded. "I actually need a few extra minutes to finish feeding my son and prepare him for bed anyway. Just ring the bell when you get here, and I'll buzz you in."

"Okay, great!" Andrew responded. "I really appreciate it. See you in a few minutes."

Andrew hung the phone up as he readied himself to meet with the first member of the church's finance committee. Even though Andrew said he would be late, he was actually early. He had been parked around the corner from her apartment for over an hour, going over his presentation notes. That was just his way of controlling the situation, by making it seem as if it was no big deal whether they met or not.

As he stepped out of his car, two ladies walking by complimented Andrew on how handsome he looked. He turned and told them thank you without disrupting his stride as he said aloud, "I hope Mia thinks the same!"

On a mission to secure a new client, Andrew was dressed a lot sharper than usual today, even stopping at the mall earlier to buy some new cologne. This was, after all, a meeting with Mia, who was a dentist and a single parent of a 4-year-old little boy.

His game plan was the same one he used with every other single mother he had closed before. Capitalize on the fact that the women were looking for a good man. Knowing that the women probably had their hearts broken in the past by a jerk like him, he focused on coming across as the perfect gentlemen, whose life mission was to help the "Damsels in Distress" properly plan for their and their children's financial future. He even bought stuffed animals and other gifts for the kids, knowing that the easy road to the mother's heart was through their children.

After the women let their guards down, Andrew would then take advantage of his good looks and start flirting with the ladies, who at this point could not believe a man as handsome, successful, and honorable as Andrew would be the least bit interested in them. The women, not wanting to lose out on what they believed to be a good chance with Andrew, would then agree to anything he suggested, and then tell their closest friends about him. It was not by mistake that most of his clientele were women.

Andrew walked up the stairs to the building and took a deep breath before ringing the bell. "Who is it?" the voice asked through the intercom.

"Hey, Mia. It's me, Andrew!"

After she buzzed him in, he started the short journey to the fourth floor. His heart was racing from the excitement of pitching a new deal to an unsuspecting prospect. As he reached the door to his prey's apartment, Andrew took a few seconds to collect himself before he knocked. When the door opened, all he could think of when he looked at what was standing in front of him was, *Damn!*

She was obviously as excited to meet with Andrew as he was to meet with her. This was not the stressed out, tired-looking single mother that wore her faded dentist uniform everywhere she went. Here, standing in front of Andrew, was the most beautiful woman he had seen in a long time.

"Wow, you look great, Mia!"

"You don't look too shabby yourself! You'd better hurry up and come in before the neighbors start talking!"

They both laughed as Andrew entered the apartment and handed Mia the gift he bought for her son.

"Aw, my son will be so happy to see this when he wakes up. You didn't have to do that!"

"My pleasure, Mia; you've got yourself one great kid there."

She reached out to give him a hug, and Andrew could feel Mia's body relax as they embraced, then he heard the unmistakable sound of her taking a whiff of his cologne.

"Wow, you smell great!" she acknowledged as they released.

"Thanks, but I don't know how to take that; you sound and look surprised!"

"No, not surprised at all!"

"Here, let's go to the kitchen so we can talk." Mia suggested.

"Ok, lead the way!" Andrew responded.

Mia turned to go to the kitchen as Andrew's adrenaline started pumping. He followed her down the hall and had a feeling of déjà vu.

This was exactly how the meetings with the many women before Mia that he had secured as clients had started. As they turned to go into the kitchen, Andrew thought to himself, *She's mine!*

"We knew God sent you to us for something." –Mrs. Carey

On cloud nine from his successful meeting with Mia the day before, Andrew headed to the home of another finance committee member. Mr. Carey and his wife Linda had been married for 22 years, and were only a couple of years away from retirement.

This was a huge opportunity for Andrew. With so many baby boomers entering retirement, he would capitalize greatly by landing the right client, who would then advocate on his behalf to their other baby boomer friends. It was a fail-proof plan.

Strangely, Andrew had never examined the Carey's unique financial situation before, but he felt confident that they would agree with the proposal he developed for their issues. Actually, it was the same proposal he used with every other couple he pitched that was going into retirement. His thoughts were that everyone needed the same thing in retirement, which was guaranteed income. So all he did was change the names at the top of the proposal to reflect who he was soliciting at the time.

Andrew used the same game plan over and over again when he dealt with the retirement market. Knowing the bad reputation financial professionals had, and the volatility of the markets, along with the negative reports from the banks, he figured he would capitalize on the fear the baby boomers had of doing something, and the anxiety they had of knowing they hadn't done enough to fund their retirement.

Andrew pulled up in front of the Carey's home and parked his car. Ten minutes elapsed when he heard a voice call out for him. "Hey, Andrew, is that you? What are you waiting for? Come on in!"

As Andrew walked onto the porch, he greeted Mr. Carey and said, "Thank you. I really appreciate you meeting with me. I read about the distrust you had of financial advisors on the questionnaire I asked you to fill out, so I did not want to start off on the wrong foot by knocking on your door more than twenty minutes before our scheduled meeting."

"Oh, Andrew, that's no problem at all. It's not you I distrust; it's the terrible reports of how many advisors constantly put their own interests before their client's needs, and I must say, that concerns us."

"Yeah, there is no denying the fact that it's criminal what some of my fellow advisors are getting away with doing. Unfortunately, their actions are causing wonderful people like yourselves to become paralyzed with fear from seeking the professional advice you need. That not only jeopardizes *your* financial future, but those who may depend on you as well, and for that, I apologize!"

"That's very noble of you, Andrew, but you don't have to apologize. We know you are nothing like those predators we hear about in the news every day. The fact that Pastor James has appointed you head of the finance committee gives us the confirmation we need, so make yourself comfortable while I get my wife… Linda!"

While Mr. Carey was off getting his wife, Andrew scanned the living room for information he could use during his presentation. When they returned, Andrew stood to greet Mrs. Carey. After a few minutes of catching up, Andrew pointed to a family portrait hanging over the fireplace and said, "You have quite a beautiful family!"

"Why, thank you," responded Mr. Carey, "but that is just us with our three daughters. We also have a younger son."

He then grabbed a photo off the coffee table and handed it to Andrew.

"Wow, he looks just like you, Mr. Carey!"

Mr. Carey smiled while answering, "I hope that's a good thing!"

They all laughed, then Andrew asked, "Is he in college?"

Mr. Carey responded, "No, he graduated last summer. But he is finding it difficult to find a job in his field."

"He's working a few hours a week at his friend's non-profit, but the little money he makes is not enough to pay his monthly bills, so we are helping him until he gets on his feet."

Not really caring, but feeling that this was the perfect time to seize the moment, Andrew asked, "What did he get his degree in?"

"History," Mrs. Carey answered.

Thinking to himself, *What an idiot; who gets a degree in history?* Andrew then asked, "What are his career aspirations?"

"He wants to teach," Mr. Carey replied.

Poor kid wants to be overworked and underpaid! he thought before stating,

"That's great, because we currently have open teaching positions with my firm. It's not children he's teaching, it's financial professionals; and he'll have to get a few licenses to do it, but I can tell from talking to the two of you that he's a smart kid, and it would be no problem. And I'm sure the money he'd make would be more than he ever imagined."

"Just let me know, and I'll make the call to human resources."

"Or better yet, you've got enough on your plate; just have him give me a call himself, and I'll take care of him."

"Oh, that would be great!" Mrs. Carey answered, while hugging her husband in excitement. "We knew God sent you to us for something!"

"No, God sent you to me!" Andrew responded with a humble smile.

Andrew never planned on helping the Carey's son, because he didn't care to. His firm didn't even hire instructors unless they worked successfully in the field first. It was all a lie to get them to trust him, and from the look of things, it worked.

Feeling he had total control of the situation, Andrew went into attack mode, asking, "So tell me, what scares you two the most about retirement?"

"I'm the Pied Piper of the community." –Andrew

It was late Wednesday morning, and Andrew had just sat down at his desk to do some research when he heard a very distinctive voice. When he looked up he saw John Cummings walking by in his tailor-made suit with a French-cuffed shirt and diamond cufflinks matching his Rolex watch.

John was a senior advisor who had been with the firm for nearly 15 years and had a book of business he'd built to die for. He no longer prospected for new business; because of his impeccable reputation as a trusted advisor, the business just came to him. He'd worked hard as a junior advisor, developing his product knowledge and securing the top industry licenses possible. And because of that, he was now reaping the rewards of his efforts.

In Andrew's mind, he was better now, and would become more successful than John Cummings at an earlier age, because he focused strictly on prospecting and did not waste time increasing product knowledge. They had support from product specialists at his firm. Nor did he plan on attaining any additional licenses, because he felt he didn't need them. "That shit takes too much time away from me building my book of business!" he would always say.

John turned his head in the direction of Andrew and noticed what was on his computer screen. To Andrew's surprise, John asked, "Andrew, why are you always wasting your time on that Facebook crap when you're supposed to be prospecting?"

"It's the island of opportunities," Andrew answered.

Laughing, John responded as he disappeared around the corner, "And you, too have an opportunity to end up right where they are; on Fantasy Island. You rookies have a long way to go!"

Andrew turned in both directions, becoming relieved that no one had witnessed the embarrassing exchange. Andrew was not mad; actually, he understood John's point of view. On his page alone he could see a friend posting pictures of the 20 pairs of Jordan basketball shoes he and his wife bought their 3-year-old daughter, but knew they lived paycheck to paycheck, because they asked to borrow money from him not too long ago. And there were others bragging about how successful they'd become and how much money they'd made, but from his experience, those who really *were* wealthy had more sense than time to be on Facebook bragging about the riches they had amassed.

The fact that most of his friends on Facebook were unsophisticated when it came to personal finance made it more and more appealing to Andrew. He did not have to have great product knowledge or other credentials. All he had to do was appear sincere in helping them through their situation, earning their trust. Instead of going after highly paid and highly educated prospects that every other advisor was going after and that would challenge his ability, he chose to focus on the low-hanging fruit in his circle that no one wanted to touch.

I'm the Pied Piper of the community! Andrew thought to himself.

Andrew was suddenly interrupted by the ringing of his cell phone. He did not recognize the number, so he let it go to voicemail. When he listened to the message, he was relieved when he found out who the call was from.

"Scrub might earn his keep after all!" he thought, as he wrote down the information left on his voicemail before deleting the message. It was Henry, the down-on-his-luck son of Mr. and Mrs. Carey who left the message. Andrew met with Henry last week and convinced him, with the promise of a cash payout, to make a warm introduction to Warren, his childhood friend and new executive director of Orion's Mission, the most popular nonprofit in the city. Warren just replaced his older brother as head of the organization after he was elected to the city council.

"Man, getting involved with this organization will give instant access to the power brokers of the city!" he thought with excitement.

After going to the vending machine for a late breakfast, Andrew returned to his desk to finish his research. He logged back into Facebook and typed in the search field the name Scott left on his voicemail, ORION'S MISSION.

Aw, there it is, just as I expected, he thought to himself, while scrolling through the many pictures on Orion's Mission's Facebook page. "Young guys who love to party!" *This is going to be like taking candy from a baby!* he thought, as he picked up the phone to confirm with Warren the time of their meeting Henry left on his voicemail.

"It's show time." –Andrew

It was a mild, gloomy Thursday, with the forecast of heavy thundershowers; but Andrew still found himself at the carwash, washing his car. In two hours he was scheduled to meet Warren, the executive director of Orion's Mission, and his board members, who held the key to his prosperity.

Tapping into this market would open the flood gates of opportunity for Andrew, who would be exposed to the cut-throat political scene of the city. All he had to do now was convince them that signing on as a client was the best decision they could make to move the organization forward.

While most advisors in his position would have done extensive research in preparation for the meeting, being a true master of the moment, all Andrew did was look at a few pictures on Facebook to see what role he had to play.

He could tell from the pictures on their page that everyone in the organization was fairly young and somehow related, so his plan was to impress them with his look of success and capitalize on their inexperience.

As he pulled into the parking lot, the space right in front of Orion's Mission's office became available. He slowly started to park when he noticed movement from the shadows behind the curtain. It was just as Andrew wanted; he could tell that everyone in the office was staring at him through the window.

Andrew grabbed his briefcase as he exited the car and then entered the office attempting to introduce himself to the receptionist. "Good morning my-" and before he could get his name out, a voice called from the conference room, "Nice ride!"

"Thank you," Andrew responded.

"What is it?"

"It's the new Porsche Panamera."

"Damn, that's sweet!"

Even though he knew who he was, Andrew acted like he didn't. He walked towards the young man and said, "I'm Andrew Johnson."

"I know who you are; you're everything Henry described. I'm Warren, the new executive director."

"Wow, it's great to finally putting a face to the name. I really appreciate the kind words. I hope I can live up to the hype!" Andrew responded with a smile.

"The pleasure is all mine. My board and I are very excited to meet with you! We hear you are going to lead us to the Promised Land!"

"Let's just say, I'll take your organization places you've never dreamed of going!" Andrew responded in a cool and confident tone.

"Well, lead the way!" Warren stated with excitement. "But first, come on; let me introduce you to the board."

As Andrew turned to follow Warren into the board room he thought to himself, *It's show time!*

Andrew was suddenly jerked out of his daze by the unexplained sensation of falling from the sky. *What the hell was that?* he asked himself. *Was I dreaming?* When he realized his reality, he wished he was dreaming. *Wow, if I'd only made better decisions with my life, I would not be living this nightmare!* he thought to himself.

He soon had the strange feeling that every eye in the room was focused on him. Hoping no one noticed his embarrassing moment, he mustered up enough courage to scan the room. *I wish Grandpa could be here,* he thought to himself.

Andrew sadly turned back around and reached for a notepad and pencil as he secretly sketched to pass the time. A few minutes passed before Andrew's mind started to wander again, replaying a day that started off as one of the best days of his life, but ended as the worst day ever.

"Fake it till you make it." –Andrew

"Great selection, sir. So now all I have to do is print the lease agreement for you to sign, and we will be done. Do you have any last questions?"

"Yes, I'm not feeling well. Where is your restroom?"

"Down the hall past the vending machine on the left. It's actually by the printer, so just follow me."

When Andrew turned to watch his grandfather and the finance manager exit the office, he noticed the many eyes fixed on his every move. The normal reaction would be, "Why are all these strangers staring at me?" However, he knew who and why all eyes and attention was on him.

When they returned, they finalized the transaction. As they stood to leave, the finance manager said,

"Welcome to the family. It's been a pleasure doing business with you!"

"Thank you; you're a kind young man!" Andrew's grandfather responded.

As the three walked out of the office, the finance manager asked,

"So, Andrew; you still in the mortgage business?"

Andrew replied with a smug smile as he pulled out one of his business cards. "I am what you consider a jack of all trades, so feel free to call me if you need anything!"

Life was great for Andrew. In just two short weeks after getting his last car repossessed, he steered his new Mercedes Coup onto the street his apartment is on. It isn't the nicest of neighborhoods, with its foreclosed standalones and rundown tenements. There had been promise here a couple of years ago when Andrew first moved in with Corrine, his girlfriend. But when the economy went south, the various condo and townhouse projects lost funding and left their developments standing as skeletal monuments to the dire financial times. Not that it bothered Andrew, necessarily. He would never make a commitment on a mortgage. He rented, had always rented, and would probably always rent. In his mind it wasn't about equity, it was about appearances.

It's for that reason that Andrew rolled so slowly down the block. He wanted everyone to get a chance to look at his new Coup. He was in sales, after all, and in sales, it often helps to look the part of success. His motto was, "Fake it till you make it!" And lately he had been doing more faking than making. He remained confident that there were a couple of huge deals coming down the pipeline soon, especially if his lousy brother would just introduce him to his new teammates in Europe.

Business had been terribly slow lately. Andrew joined many different groups to solicit his business, but for some reason, the well had run dry. There was a time not long ago when closing a deal was just a matter of visiting someone in the family, or at least friendly with the family. Nowadays, he found every call running cold.

For months, he'd been blaming the economy for his struggles. Blaming the economy for keeping him in what was supposed to be a temporary apartment for more than two years now. Blaming the economy for keeping him from moving into that luxury apartment downtown, the one Corrine reminded him about every night of the week. Blaming the economy for preventing him from earning more money so he could pay off his creditors. None of his financial struggles had to do with his work habits or bad money management.

There were many advisors in his office who never showed up for work before 10:00, and never stayed past 4:00. Some of them even played golf twice a week. As far as he knew, none of their cars or homes were leased using their grandparents' names. In Andrew's mind, the reason his colleagues had gotten to where they were was simply because "they always look the part!"

Grandpa's help or not, it had been especially gratifying to lease his car from this Mercedes dealership. Andrew had worked there once. It had been his first job after dropping out of college. He fancied himself to be a great salesman, and out of the gate he sold a few cars to family and friends; but by the end of his time there, he was unceremoniously fired for putting the dealership at risk by misleading customers, not to mention his lagging sales numbers. It had been the economy then, too. "How can a guy sell cars when the whole country is too strapped to even go out to eat anymore?" he stated as justification before being fired. That's why it felt unexplainably satisfying to lease his Mercedes from the same jerk who had laughed at him after his termination six years ago. *Talking about are you still in*

the mortgage business! You don't care is what I should've said to that bum!
Andrew thought, while flashing a smile at his neighbor's young son
as he gawked from his yard across the street. He then made the slow
turn into his driveway.

"Aw, hell. I don't have time for this shit!" he said out loud.

His heart sank when he saw a familiar person waiting for him on the
doorstep, totally ruining the moment. It was Mr. Davis, and from the
look on his sagging, wrinkled, pudgy face, he'd come to ask about
the overdue rent. Andrew tried to look coy as he threw the car into
park. He attempted to resemble a man terribly forgetful about the rent
that was due. But in truth, he knew very well that his rent was more
than two weeks late.

"Nice car," Mr. Davis stated when Andrew stepped out.

"Appreciate it, just got it today," Andrew replied. "I picked it up at
this dealership where I used to work. They gave me a great deal!"

"Is that why you are late again on the rent?"

Andrew sighed. He had been expecting this, but truly old man
Davis was in a particularly sour mood.

"Because that car you just bought says you've got money. I don't
know anyone who drives a Mercedes that is broke!" Mr. Davis added.

Andrew shook his head, trying to look repentant. "I didn't buy it;
my grandparents leased it for me."

Strangely, Mr. Davis started laughing. "Is that supposed to make
me feel better? Let me get this straight; your rent is almost a month
late, but instead of paying off your obligation to me, you go out and
rent something else?"

"I'm not renting it," Andrew said as he raised his eyebrows. "I'm
leasing it."

The old landlord's laugh became wild and boisterous.

"What's so funny?" Andrew asked.

"Aren't you supposed to be a financial advisor?" Mr. Davis asked
sarcastically, while struggling to catch his breath from all of the laughter. His face reddened, as he squinted his eyes tight and continued. "I
mean, how do you expect your clients to take your financial advice if

you don't? Not knowing that leasing is the same as renting is scary. Are you sure you're qualified for your job?"

As Andrew started to reply, he was abruptly cut off—"It's a rhetorical question. That's not my problem; I just want my damn money! I feel sorry for the uninformed fool who trusts you enough to follow your advice over the bridge to nowhere!"

Suddenly Andrew lost it and shouted, "I couldn't care less about my clients! I'm only in the business for the money!"

As Andrew stopped he felt his adrenaline flow through his veins as his anger rose. He couldn't help but notice all the eyes on the street looking at him and Mr. Davis.

There were a large number of people outside on this unusually warm afternoon, and his landlord's volume about the missing rent was getting a little too loud for Andrew's liking. As if the old man could read his thoughts, he stopped cackling and responded,

"That's right. I know you've got the money, Andy."

Andrew started seething, because he hated being called 'Andy', and the old man knew it.

"Your brother is a big basketball star; why don't you just call him? He might help you out. Poor cocky Mercedes-driving Andy needs a bailout," Mr. Davis sang as he shook his head.

The mention of his younger brother, let alone the public mockery by Mr. Davis, was causing Andrew's face to blush with fury. It took all of his restraint not to hit the crusty old man. If he wasn't worried about the odds of finding a new apartment on his credit and scraping together enough money for a security deposit and moving crew, he wouldn't care so much about Mr. Davis' wellbeing. If the economy wasn't so bad, he'd clock the old man and pack his bags. As it was, Andrew knew he must beat back his anger and take on a more placating tact.

"As it happens, Mr. D.," Andrew said in a softer, more controlled tone, "I have a meeting lined up with one of Bobby's new teammates next week." This was a flat-out lie, but that didn't matter in this moment. "When that deal goes through, I'll pay you not just the money I owe, but for the next six months in advance. How does that sound?"

To Andrew's surprise, the old man's eyes went wide. He couldn't believe it, but Mr. Davis appeared to be buying the lie he just told him. Mr. Davis assumed the same expression Andrew was taught to look for during his many hours of sales training. The one that indicates a prospect or client was sold on the sales pitch. It had been such a long time since he had seen it in anyone that he almost forgot what it looked like. In response, he tried to look and sound nonchalant, just as he was taught.

"He's the highest-paid player in Europe," Andrew said, as he crossed his arms over his chest after telling his landlord the player's name.

Mr. Davis slumped, chewing his lip as if in deep thought. Andrew could tell that he was winning him over a little more with every second he allowed to pass in silence. This was part of his training as well. When a prospect thinks, you keep your mouth shut. Slowly, the old man began to nod. Andrew tried to foster the nod with an even more aloof posture. He threw his head back as if inspecting the roof of his apartment.

"Okay."

Andrew quickly stepped forward and offered his hand for shaking. Mr. Davis took it hesitantly, but his grip was firm in the end.

"You know I'm a man of my word!"

"Yeah, yeah," Mr. Davis responded, as he limped down the driveway to his car.

"I rented to the wrong brother," he mumbled as he departed. With the parting jab he just received from his landlord, Andrew's ire returned. He reminded himself again that this was one man with whom you don't argue. He diffused his anger by counting in his head all the ways he had beaten his brother in life.

Bobby doesn't have a Mercedes Coup; he drives a lousy Beamer. And though Andrew has never been invited to his brother's home in Madrid, he bet he didn't have a flat screen in every room, like he does. By the time he unlocked the door to his apartment, Andrew's mood changed as he laughed. *Hell, I even have a flat screen in the bathroom, I win!* he thought, with a smile on his face. "Rented to the wrong brother my ass old man!" he screamed as he slammed the door shut.

Stepping through the door, Andrew found his lavishly furnished apartment exactly as he'd left it. The maids had done their work well, as they always do every Friday. He was home earlier than usual, because he wanted to beat Corrine. He needed enough time to set up and wrap the gift he'd bought for her. She had been on his case recently on how he hadn't been pulling his weight maintaining his share of the bills, so he wanted to surprise her with what he thought to be a satisfying gift.

She would get plenty of appeasement from her new iPad. It cost Andrew almost his entire paycheck, but it was worth it. He justified to himself that it didn't matter that they had one already. Even though it's rarely used, it's almost a year old, and the new one just came out. Now she'll have her own and it'll be nicer and newer of the two. They each had their own laptops, so having to share an iPad had been a terrible inconvenience. *That inconvenience ends today!* he thought to himself as he smiled.

He was so excited about the thought of how she would react that he allowed himself to think wishfully. Even though his feelings for Corrine were forced, and maybe he was not as attracted to her as he used to be, she was all he had. With his bad credit and limited income, it would be impossible, in his mind, to attract the type of woman he really wanted. "It's easier staying with someone who knows your flaws even if you're unhappy, than it is to start over!" he'd always convinced himself.

Maybe she'll be so happy that she won't remind him of what she's reminded him of every night for months. Maybe he could avoid hearing about how it's his fault they still live in this neighborhood.

As he passed in the direction of his bedroom, he snatched up his universal remote control. In his bedroom, he used the remote to switch on the flat screen. He flipped through a few channels before stopping on the one connected to his surveillance system. There's no real reason to watch this channel, or to have had the system installed to begin with. He focused less about the peace of mind it brought Corrine, and more about how much it impressed his friends.

As he turned to go sit on his memory foam bed, he noticed something on the edge of the mahogany nightstand. That is where Corrine piles his bills, because he tends to forget about them if they aren't left right next to where he sleeps. The pile is especially large today, with the middle of the month approaching. He scanned through the top few envelopes, tossing them aside when they had "second notice" and "failure to pay" stamps near the lip.

He opened what appeared to be a letter from an attorney. It was a notification that he was being sued by another driver he collided with after trying to run a red light. Andrew had just let his insurance lapse a week before to lower his monthly auto expenses, and was subsequently ticketed by the police at the scene of the accident.

He put the letter down as he shook his head and continued to scan, when he saw a familiar envelope from the hospital that treated him after the accident. He tore it open, expecting to find the reduction in the bill he had demanded over the phone a few weeks back. When he saw that his request had been denied and the massive sum he was charged was being classified as bad debt and assigned to a collections agency, he scoffed and mumbled to himself as he tossed the bill into the trash, "It wasn't my fault she slammed on her brakes. I'm not paying a red cent."

Coincidentally, the envelope next in the stack was an offer for health insurance. Andrew blasted air through his teeth, amused. "I'm too healthy for that right now," he said, tossing the letter in the trash atop his unpaid medical bill. As he made his way to the closet for wrapping paper, he snickered, thinking about the advice his grandfather once gave him. "Insurance maybe a great way to make money, but it's also a huge waste of money!"

After wrapping the gift, Andrew stepped out of the closet when he heard the front door open and close.

"You're home early!" Andrew yelled.

Excitedly, he stepped out from the bedroom, holding Corrine's gift behind his back. "Hello, baby. See the new car?"

"Is that really yours, or did you trick another one of your so-called friends into letting you use theirs?"

"No, it's mine! All I need to get now are some rims!"

"What 30-plus-year-old man in his right mind gets a luxury car like that and tricks it out with rims? Wow, you're such a stereotype!" she yelled as she rolled her eyes at him while striding down the hall in his direction. "I'm not even going to *ask* how you got a car like that so soon after you had your last one repossessed!"

"Why do you always want to focus on the negative by dwelling on the past? I made a mistake!" he acknowledged, before backing out of her way so she could pass. He held the iPad carefully behind his back, preserving the surprise. "If you're really good, I'll give you a ride later."

Corrine rose up on her toes and pecked him on the cheek. "Oh yeah? You think we could ride past the apartment building downtown while we're out?"

Andrew was pissed now. Corrine hadn't been home more than five minutes, and already she'd reminded him of the apartment he had failed to deliver her.

"Because I just received a call from the lady in their rental office," she continued, as she walked into the bedroom. "She says she can show us that three-bedroom apartment if we can get down there by six."

With a sigh, Andrew wheeled around the corner with the gift still pressed behind his back. He tried to make his smile look genuine, but the truth was that he was thoroughly annoyed as he thought to himself, *Once I get my shit in order, I'm leaving her ass!*

He watched as Corrine slipped out of her work dress and started digging into the closet for something more comfortable to wear. "I got you a present," he said.

She stopped what she was doing and stood to her full alluring height. The look on her lovely face was a combination of excitement and disapproval. Andrew had seen this look many times before. Every time he had ever come home with a new purchase or rental, he had received it. By now, it doesn't even bother him.

Before she could respond, he swung the gift around from behind his back and held it out to her. With a light hop in her step, she drifted to him and took it. He delighted in the moment that her eyes brightened in anticipation, but the moment was short-lived. His cell phone rang, snapping his attention away from her. Normally he would let it go to voicemail, but this is the ringtone that came through when his boss calls.

He held up a finger to Corrine, requesting that she wait. She ignored him and took the gift over to the bed to unwrap it.

"Hello?" Andrew said into the phone, his attention half on the call and half scanning for his girlfriend's reaction.

"How many times have I advised you not to answer your phone so casually?"

Andrew groaned inwardly. He had hoped that it wasn't Ryan, his sales manager. But it was Ryan, and he sounded angry.

"Sorry, Ryan, I don't answer my phone like this when it's a prospect or client, I promise, man."

"Whatever. Listen, dude!" Ryan barked. "That's not why I'm calling, anyway. You remember that Smith deal?"

Andrew nodded into the phone, though he knew it was silly to do so. He recalled the deal very well. It had led to a $50k advance that had paid for all the amazing new televisions and wiring in the apartment. There had even been enough for the security system. It had taken the promise of an additional $45k that would come once the second deal closed to convince Corrine that buying all the equipment was a good investment. But now, as his nerves rose slowly, he still believed it to be money well spent. His apartment was now the talk of the town. Impressing everyone he invited to his apartment was how a successful salesman raises his profile.

"Well, sit down, Andrew, because *both* deals have fallen through!"

Andrew experienced for the first time in his life why people always tell you to sit down when they have bad news. His legs became weak.

Woozily, he dropped back into the hallway wall, barely catching himself before he fell completely. It took him a moment to collect himself enough to respond, and when he did his voice came out in a crackling whisper. "They fell through?"

"Yes, he and his wife changed their minds! Didn't you say he was a good friend of yours?" Ryan asked. "What type of people do you have in your circle?"

Andrew stood up as his mind started reeling. He had been counting on the two deals to help get him above water. Smitty is what they called him when they were younger. He was one of Andrew's best friends in college, and the guy is loaded. He has the cars, the homes, and the clothes of a high-paid executive.

Andrew sold him on two, five-million dollar life insurance annuities for him and his wife, which was more than they needed. But because of his high income level and their past relationship, Smitty asked no questions. Andrew had been so excited to make the sell that he practically ran back to the office with the check in hand.

"But I collected his payment myself!" Andrew assured his boss.

"His wife put a stop payment on it, you idiot! She said the signature on the application was not hers!"

"Oh," Andrew responded, sliding back down the wall, sitting on the floor.

Corrine chose this moment to step into the hallway. The way she looked at him, it was clear she could sense a problem. Andrew felt his face flush and his hands go numb.

"So, um," he managed. "What um, what do we do?"

There was a long, crippling silence from the other end of the line.

"Mrs. Smith has accused you of forging her signature; is she right?"

"She was not available for a couple of weeks, and I only had two days to close the deal in order to get paid that month. So I figured since her husband had agreed to the terms, that it wasn't a big deal! So yes, I did sign her name on the contract."

Ryan yelled with such force that Andrew could feel the air through the phone. "Are you crazy? It's one thing to sacrifice your future over a few thousand dollars; but to put the company at risk of fines and penalties is not acceptable! You were fortunate that we were in need of warm bodies when we hired you, because my gut told me not to, after hearing about your deceptive track record in both the auto and mortgage industries. I should have listened.

"Andrew, in light of what I've just learned, you are ordered to immediately return the $50k advance you received from us! Have your ass in my office tomorrow at eight, or I'll have the cops looking for you, because this conversation is not over!" *Click...*

All at once, a half-dozen conflicting emotions assaulted Andrew's mind, as he struggled to ponder his options. He didn't have the money, had no way to get the money, nor did he even have a bank account.

Not even Corrine knows this fact. He cringed at the thought of finally having to reveal this embarrassing secret to her. He hadn't had an account in over a year now, because he was trying to avoid having his account frozen by the IRS. Sure, he paid what most consider predatory fees at various check cashing places to cash his commission checks; but losing a percentage of his check was a lot better than having all of his money seized by the government.

The feeling of terror overwhelmed him at that moment.

"What is it?" Corrine asked, her tone bordering between concern and anger.

Andrew drew a long breath as if to speak, but he held his silence. He knew he would need some time to gather himself and plot his words carefully. Corrine, to her credit, gave him some space. Blessed with the brief silence, he thought about all the potential ways out of this jam. He could file bankruptcy again. It was easy last time. He had basically washed his hands of over $60,000 in credit card debt by just filling out some paperwork. But he suddenly remembered reading something recently about how bankruptcy has been a different animal since 2005.

Then he remembered his business idea. If it's not too late, he could set up that credit repair service full-time. There's literally no overhead. Just a website and an online payment portal, and the work in the business is very minimal. And the most appealing aspect is that the results are not guaranteed.

He could continue financial advising by day, and increase his focus on the credit repair business on the side. The hope this thought brought him lasted only for an instant when he considered how many years it would take him to repay $50,000 with a small-time side business.

Then it hit him. *Nothing else matters. If I'm charged with fraud, I'll lose everything, maybe even my freedom!* he thought to himself, as tears started to form.

"I'm in trouble, Corrine. I've got to pay them back."

"Pay who back?" she asked.

He explained the harrowing situation, and with every passing syllable, her eyes grew darker, and her expression tightened. By the time he was finished, it was a struggle to even look her in the eye.

She tossed the iPad at his feet and said, as she stomped to the closet to get her jacket, "Well, I guess you can start with this!"

"We're never getting out of this hell hole, are we?" she asked.

She didn't wait for a reply. Furiously, she ran out the front door, slamming it behind her. Andrew was left standing in the hallway, all alone, with an iPad at his feet.

"Yes, I'm in deep trouble!" –Andrew

Andrew walked off the elevator on his way to meet with Ryan. Not knowing exactly what to expect, the closer he got to his boss' office, the more and more butterflies formed in his belly, and the more lightheaded he became.

Before he could knock on the door he heard,

"Come on in and close the door, Andy, so I can tell you what your problem is!"

The manager leaned forward, tenting his hands in front of his face as Andrew took a seat.

"You're lazy."

His jaw clenched reflexively. Andrew did his best not to fly into a rage. He had been called many things by lesser people, but to be called— lazy.

"That's right," Ryan stressed. "Lazy." The manager paused, apparently for dramatic effect. He leaned back in his chair and looked slowly from the left to the right. "I'll bet you're sitting there thinking you are in this tight spot because of bad luck—but do you really want to know the truth? I've got 17 financial advisors in this office that I know are 100% ethical, and would never forge anyone's signature on a contract in an attempt to get paid sooner. You know why?"

Andrew began to feel a lump form in the back of his throat. He knew that if he spoke now, it would come out as a scream. Instead, he swallowed carefully.

"Because they have other deals in the pipeline, you lazy, selfish bastard!" Ryan screamed as he rose from his chair. "Any other decent advisor wouldn't have needed the advance in the first place. They would've also had the money to pay us back if they had to!"

The manger held up two fingers, smiling condescendingly. "Two reasons for that, son. First, they've got the money in the bank from all the other deals they've closed. Secondly, they wouldn't be so stupid to go out and spend money they don't yet have. An advance is just that; you've got to earn it before you spend it. As a financial advisor, you should know that!"

"Do you have a clue what I did last night?" Ryan asked.

A puzzled Andrew responded,

"No."

"I stayed here until two this morning, going through your desk and auditing every single one of your files with the compliance department. We've discovered a deeper level of deceit than the Smith deal from the many complaint letters you were foolish enough to keep in your drawer. You see, you were so lazy that you left a paper trail in your drawer, you pathetic piece of shit!"

Finally reaching his boiling point, Andrew lifted his six-foot-two frame out of the chair and hovered over his five-foot-five boss and screamed, "I don't have to take this shit! Say something else and I will knock your ass out!"

Andrew then turned and rushed out of the building. He got in his car and rolled out of the driveway, the Mercedes' white paint sparkling the moment the hood passed into the sunlight. Using the voice recognition on his phone, he called his grandparents' number. When the line picked up, his grandmother's voice rang loudly through the car's speakers.

"Hey, Gram," Andrew said, trying to sound as pleasant and worry-free as possible as he dropped the pet name his grandmother had always enjoyed.

"Andrew, my boy!" Grandma Fran said. "Why, we were just talking about you."

"Well, can I blame you?" Andrew said, laying it on thick.

His grandmother chuckled. "How's that lovely girlfriend of yours?"

"Hey, Gram?" Andrew said, feeling a little sorry to cut his grandmother off. "Can you put Grandpa on?"

In the silence that followed, Andrew could practically hear his grandmother's thoughts. They sounded startled at first. Then worried. And then, all too knowing. "I'll put him on," she said, her tone unsurprised.

Andrew can't blame her. He has made this kind of call before.

"Hey, son," came the voice of his grandpa. "How's that Mercedes treating you?"

Andrew tried to laugh it off. "Runs like a dream," he answered. "You should know, you drove it!"

"How else did you think you would get me to sign on the dotted line?" Grandpa responded. "If I'm committing to lease a Mercedes, even if you are paying it off next month, you'd better believe I'm gonna take it for a spin from time to time." Grandpa paused, sounding as if he was laughing himself. "In fact, it's been about 24 hours or so. Why don't you swing by so I can have a little refresher?"

Andrew would laugh if he weren't so tense. "Grandpa," he said with a deep sigh, wishing he had taken some time to compose a speech before making this call. He cursed himself under his breath for being in this position.

"You need some money," Grandpa said directly.

Andrew was so shocked that it took him a moment to process the words his grandfather just spoke. He knew he had made this call before, but it couldn't possibly have been so many times that his grandfather could sense it.

"I know the whole song and dance by now, son," Grandpa said, interrupting Andrew's train of thought. "In fact, we've kind of been expecting this call since yesterday."

Andrew felt breathless. "You have?"

"Sure," Grandpa said, his voice sounding surprisingly lighthearted. "Every time you get yourself into some hot water, you make a huge purchase. It's like you try to convince yourself you aren't in trouble by buying something you can't afford."

"That's not true!" Andrew responded defiantly.

"Oh? So you're not calling about money, then?"

Andrew's heart sank. This is the last place he wanted to be with his grandfather; he had lost control of the conversation. He meant to call and explain to his grandparents the trouble he'd found himself in, dealing with the wrong type of clients. But by now, his mind was so tied up in knots that he had forgotten the lie he'd prepared.

"Yes, I'm in deep trouble," he finally admitted.

"What?" Grandpa answered. "It can't be that bad. I'm sure everything will work itself out like it always has!"

A sudden tear slid over Andrew's cheek. "No, not this time, Grandpa." He tried to hide the fact that he was crying, but it was clear that he had failed.

"What's going on that has you so distraught?"

Andrew did his best to explain. With tears falling freely, he detailed the issue with the advance, skimming over the fact that he'd spent it all on lavish items he didn't need. He explained thoroughly how his friend Smitty and his wife got cold feet so they made a false accusation about Andrew in an effort to get their money back from the firm. By the time he was finished talking, he had painted himself as an innocent victim, with the entire planet against him.

Nervously, Grandpa asked, "How does this affect the money you are using to pay the car off next month?"

"Grandpa, it's all gone; there is no money."

There was an uncomfortable silence before Andrew's grandfather responded in a saddened, nervous tone.

"I wish we could help you, son; truly, I do. But we're all tapped out."

The shock from his grandfather's response caused Andrew to become lightheaded. With his vision blurring due to the stress, he swerved briefly into the opposite lane, steering the car back on course at the sound of the horns from oncoming traffic.

"I mean…" Grandpa continued.

Andrew thought he overheard his grandmother in the background, her voice pinched as if she was arguing. Then she grabbed the phone and said sternly,

"Andrew, the only time we hear from you now is when you need rescuing from a financial crisis you've gotten yourself into! The last time we foolishly bailed you out of something, we had to take out another mortgage on our house, that we'll probably be paying on until after you retire! I, I, I warned your grandfather not to help you get that car because as always we would be left holding the bag. I didn't realize it would be so soon! We don't have any more money, and even if we did, we wouldn't give it to you!"

Fuming at the way his grandmother spoke to him and overcome with stress from the situation he was in caused Andrew to lose it and go off on his grandmother. "Who cares what you think off me; you never cared about me anyway! I'm not your perfect, little Bobby! I don't need help from you or anyone else. I will show you! Forget I ever exist--!" Before he could finish the last statement, he heard the line go dead. "Hello? Hello? Did they hang up on me?" he asked out loud. Andrew figured if he made his grandparents feel guilt and sorrow for him that they would do for him whatever he needed, like they always had; but this time was different.

It finally hit him that there was no way out of the situation, causing every inch of his body to fall numb. With the gravity of the moment overwhelming him, his eyes began to roll. His head pitched heavily to one side. He lost control of the wheel. His tires screeched. A loud crash followed. A great, black wave washed over Andrew.

As the scene was playing out like a bad movie scene in Andrew's head, he was shaken from his thoughts before it finished by a loud, deep voice.

"Andrew Johnson, please rise!"

"Do you want to make a statement on your behalf?" the voice asked.

Andrew's head started spinning as he turned to begin the most important presentation he had ever made.

"What can I say, other than I'm sorry for all of the people I've hurt over the years. I'm a good guy that made a few bad decisions under pressure, but it is what it is," he said with the look of acceptance on his face as he continued. "The best word of advice I can give is that **IN A CAPITALISTIC SOCIETY, YOU'VE GOT TO QUESTION EVERYONE'S INTENTIONS!**"

"Well said, Mr. Johnson, and I truly wish for your sake that you were ethical in your life; but unfortunately, you decided to use your power of persuasion and the trust people instilled in you to do bad things. It does not matter how good a person you claim to be. Actions speak louder than words. Your fraudulent actions and shady dealings in the finance industry, along with your tax evasion, leaves me no other option but to hereby order you to serve the maximum 48 months in prison!"

A defeated Andrew showed no emotion when he heard the judge's decision. The worst part for him was not that his life was ruined and that he had to go to prison for the desperate acts of crimes he'd committed trying to sustain a plush lifestyle, just like his father. It was the fact that no one in his family came to support him through his trying time.

Because of the selfish and deceiving actions he'd learned from his mother, Andrew was truly all alone. The courtroom erupted with joy as he was led out, with his head down, in handcuffs.

Bobby

"To give money to the irresponsible is to gamble!"
–Wise man

As his entourage lounged around the bedroom, Bobby went into his large walk-in closet to put on the clothes his new stylist Lynette had selected for him to wear at the poker table tonight. His teammates have a team tradition of holding a high-stakes game once per week, the location rotating between a venue of choice by each participant.

As a rookie, Bobby was one of the last in line to host the game, and since this was his first time, even though he felt he was better than his teammates, he knew that fitting in with them would ensure that he would stay on the team. So, he was intent on impressing them all with his outside-the-box planning for this evening's festivities.

With the help from Xavier, his agent, Bobby decided to do something he figured no one had ever thought about doing before, rent a jet to host the poker game.

"What time do we take off, X?" Bobby yelled from inside the closet.

"Seven thirty, big fella," Xavier responded.

"I can't wait to see the guys' faces when they get out of the limos I sent for them and see me standing on the top step of our private jet for tonight." Bobby stated.

"Yeah," a member of his entourage responded. "We will have the cameras rolling so we can replay that moment over and over again. Then we will upload it to YouTube. Shit, I might even leak it to one of those television shows or gossip websites to show them how real ballers do it!"

"Right, right!" Bobby responded, before stepping out of the closet with a nervous look on his face, until his entourage start yelling their approval when they saw what he was wearing.

"A polka-dotted suit and Capri pants with dress shoes and no socks? Now that's swag, home boy, that's swag!"

"Yeah, you better give Lynette a raise before she goes somewhere else, 'cause when people see you rocking that, she will be in high demand!" another entourage member yelled.

The fact is that before finally making it into the NBA, after years spent honing his skills on the European circuit, Bobby would have never been caught dead in clothes like this. But the hipster style had seemed to take hold in the league, and he'd never had a problem with playing or looking the part. Despite the fact that his contract was non-guaranteed and he could be cut from the team at any time, he had done his best to play the part in all ways.

Upon leveraging a huge mortgage, he purchased an eight-bedroom, five-bathroom estate on eleven sprawling acres of land. Every room was massive and well furnished. His six garages were filled with high-end cars, and from the front gate on the edge of his property to the front door of his house, he had lined his driveway with marble statues flown in from Italy. There was an Olympic sized infinity pool in the back yard, overlooking the makings of what would one day be a vineyard.

He smiled as he thought about the tremendous luxury in which he and his wife finally lived. As always, the smile quickly faded as he remembered what his career has cost him. For years, Bobby has struggled through a contentious relationship with his family because, from the moment he made the European league, they'd tried to take advantage of his assumed wealth. Like his grandfather showed him growing up, you think about your loved ones before you think about yourself.

Bobby had nothing to show for his years of playing overseas because he blew through all the money he made helping his family out, and also trying to impress people who thought he was rich because he was a ballplayer.

He did not care for the thought of how much money he had thrown away on his family prior to now. A wise man once told him, "To give money to the irresponsible is to gamble." And on this particular game he'd lost, time and again.

"Live and learn!" he always reasoned with himself.

Since his return to the US and a new NBA contract, their pleas had only grown stronger, particularly the ones coming from Andrew, his older brother. It seemed that he called to ask him for money every week.

Not wanting to waste this second chance at getting his life in order, Bobby decided to finally cut everyone in his family off completely. That even included his grandparents, who had always bent over backwards to support him. He figured his mother or siblings would just use them to get to him, so he wanted to avoid the drama.

He felt bad about it, but what could he do? As the youngest of the family, he'd spent his whole life with a bird's eye view of his family's egregious and deep-seated tendencies to make financial mistakes. He'd watched his grandfather, mother, and siblings dig their way into staggering holes of debt, so he paid for most things with cash to avoid those same pitfalls. He had made a declaration of living life completely different from them, and thanked God every day for giving him the physical gifts to do so.

Yes, he did walk around with large wads of cash, and he would be the first to acknowledge that he could do a better job managing his finances. But up until this point, he has never taken out more loans than his contracts could afford him.

"Hey big fella," Xavier said, as he put his arm around Bobby. "Don't forget about the meeting I scheduled for you at my firm tomorrow. We have very big plans for you!"

"X," Bobby replied, "The best advice my grandfather ever gave me was, you hire good people you trust to take care of your business, so you can focus on your other business. I can't concentrate on tonight's business, which is the poker game, if I'm focused on tomorrow's. This is what you specialize in, so I trust your decisions. Plus, you bailed me out of a serious situation, so I am forever grateful to you. That's why when you suggested I do so, I gave you the ability to make decisions and sign on my behalf, from paying my bills to signing contracts and making financial transactions. Just tell your partners I had a mandatory function with the team that I could not get out of. I'm sure they'll understand."

"No problem, Bobby, don't you worry about a thing. I got you! Oh, by the way, try not to get so close to Greg; I don't trust him."

"Thanks for the heads-up, X. I'll holla at you tomorrow."

As Xavier exited, Bobby turned and yelled out:

"C'mon fellas, let's go win us some money!"

The crew *whooped* into a jovial holler as they followed him out.

"I'm all in." –Bobby

"You should see my new seven-sixty," Bobby bragged to Greg, the team's best and highest-paid player, and also a former client of Xavier's.

"That's a BMW, right?" Greg asked, looking annoyed as he called the rookie point guard's bet.

"You know it," Bobby responded. "With all the modifications I made, that thing ended up costing me over six figures; but you should feel the way it handles."

"Got a spacious back seat too, I hear," Derek said. He's the team's sixth man, and also a bit of a womanizer.

The men laughed.

Bobby started to relish the feeling of being accepted by his more tenured peers, so he kept the ball rolling on his game of show and tell. "And look at this," he said, flashing his new watch at Greg. "It's a Patek."

Greg scowled as he batted Bobby's hand away. "Rookie, you gonna bet or what?"

"Yeah, Rook," Derek snapped. "You really think any of us are impressed with your new little toys?"

An uncomfortable silence followed. Bobby, in his nervousness at being singled out this way, let loose an audible gulp.

"Sure you had a solid career in Europe, but you've been in the big leagues, what?" Derek asked, "six weeks?"

Bobby felt his hands start to sweat as he shrugged. He was so caught up in Derek's line of questioning that he failed to notice it was his turn to bet once more. When he finally realized, without thinking, he slid a stack of chips so hard to the center that they toppled into the large pot that had formed.

"Well, I've been in the league for eight years," Derek continued. "You've got a lot of catching up to do before you can even sit at the big-boy table with me, son!"

To rub salt in the wound he just opened on Bobby, Derek made one last point.

"One more thing; Rule #1 of hosting the poker game is that it's held at a place we've never been. We've used this jet so many times that I have a free voucher for my next flight. As a matter of fact, lift your arm rest up and tell everyone what it reads."

As he focused on not looking upset at becoming the butt of the joke at his own party, a dismayed Bobby looked down at the arm rest and read loud enough for everyone to hear—"Derek was here!"

The men all laughed. "I thought we weren't gonna tell him until tomorrow, dawg," Greg yelled, as he laughed so hard he struggled to catch his breath.

Bobby was steaming as he caught sight of his entire entourage laughing at Derek's comments from the back of the room. He stewed angrily. For the first time, he decided to turn his full attention on the game. His cards were decent. He could make a straight already, and they haven't even hit the river card. He looked to his chips, finding the pile smaller than he'd remembered. It took a moment to realize the reason it had gotten so small. He'd shoved a healthy stack into the pot on his last call. His eyes darted around the table, eventually realizing that he was now alone in a one-on-one matchup with Greg. He could feel Derek's eyes measuring him up, judging him, as if his actions for the remainder of this hand would prove or disprove his worth as a man.

Bobby clenched his teeth and committed himself to winning this hand. Sure, there are three clubs on the table; but the odds of Greg having a flush are slim. More likely, he's looking for three of a kind. Bobby's straight will win.

"Your move, Rook," Greg acknowledged.

"I'm all in," Bobby responded, a little too quickly.

Everyone at the table barked their excitement. Bobby's entourage stood and approached the table to get a better look. Greg flashed a barely perceptible smile as he shoved his stack of chips in to match.

**"I guess me and the crew won't be order-
ing dessert tonight!" –Bobby**

"Yo, how much we lose last night, big homie?" one of the entourage members asked him.

"Don't worry about it, dude. What's your name, anyway?" Bobby snapped back, with a puzzled look on his face.

"They call me Q. I'm Xavier's little cousin."

"Aight cool, nice to meet you," Bobby responded, as he walked away.

"Oh yeah, one more thing," Q called out to Bobby.

"What's up, little homie?" Bobby asked, as he turned back around.

"Don't focus so much about the money you lost last night because my dad used to tell me, sometimes you have to lose to win!"

Bobby flashed a half-smile and turned around as he thought to himself,

What the hell is he talking about? It's easy to say that corny shit when it's someone else's money.

The truth is, Bobby did not want to think about how much money he'd lost. He thought maybe he entered the game with ten grand, but he couldn't remember the original buy in. Either way, whatever he lost would hurt him plenty. It was mere chump change for his more seasoned teammates, but for Bobby, he couldn't help but think about which bill he wouldn't be able to pay until next month's check.

He strode through the mall with his crew, heading for his favorite clothing store to do a little shopping like his mother used to do, to take his mind off of his problems. En route, his phone rang.

"Yeah," he answered.

"What's up, playa?" the voice asked on the other end.

"Who is this?" Bobby asked.

With laughing in the background, the voice responded,

"It's Greg, but you should call me daddy, the way I beat dat ass last night, son!"

With a halfhearted laugh, Bobby replied,

"Oh, you got jokes."

"Naw, man, on the real. I just wanted to thank you for hosting last night. We had a great time. But that's not the reason I called. I want to bless you with some insider information you may be interested in."

Puzzled at what Greg was talking about, Bobby responded,

"No problem, it was my pleasure. What information do you want to share with me?"

"My jeweler is in town meeting with me and a couple of other guys on the team. He asked if I knew of anyone else that may be interested in joining us. Peeping out your style over the last few weeks, you were the first one that came to mind. So, are you down?"

Excited at the fact that last night's debacle seemed to increase his popularity among his new teammates, Bobby responded,

"Hell, yeah, I want to order something!"

"Cool, I thought you would. Now I'm letting you know upfront so there is no problem."

"Yeah, what's up?"

"Since each piece is one of a kind, they are not cheap. He has nothing to offer less than twenty thousand dollars, which is payable at time of selection, so bring straight cash, homie."

Wow, that's steep! Bobby thought to himself. But not wanting to look bad in front of Greg, he reacted with no hesitation. "I guess me and the crew won't be ordering dessert tonight!"

Laughing, Greg replied, "Okay, cool. He'll meet us in the locker room today after practice, so we'll see you in a couple of hours."

Bobby's mind raced as he hung up the phone. "Where am I going to get twenty thousand cash by the end of practice today?"

"Shit, after all the money I lost last night, I'm barely sitting on twelve thousand, and most of that is going towards the clothes I'm buying today."

A few minutes later, as he and his entourage entered the clothing store, it hit him. *I'll just call Xavier, and get an increase on that line of credit his firm gave me*, he thought to himself.

Bobby then turned to his crew and said,

"You guys go head in, I have a quick call I need to make."

"Well let's just say, after I lace you with one of my pieces, you will be big time."
–Jules the Jeweler

"Sorry I'm late, Greg. Coach wanted to talk to me about the offense."

"No problem, Bobby. It gave me a little extra time to pick the nicest piece I've ever seen. I'm wearing it next week when we play Miami!"

"It's that nice? Bobby asked.

"Hell, yeah! After everyone sees me rocking it at the press conference, the chain will be trending by itself."

"Hold tight, Jules will be back in a few."

"Who's Jules?" Bobby asked, with a puzzled look on his face.

"The jeweler, fool!"

"No way this dude's name is Jules!" Bobby responded, while laughing.

"Yep! Jules the Jeweler is what we call him. See, here's his card."

As Bobby reached for the business card Greg was showing him, Jules the Jeweler walked in.

"You must be Big Time Bobby Johnson."

"I don't know about Big Time, but you got the Bobby Johnson right."

"Well, let's just say that after I lace you with one of my pieces, you will be Big Time."

"All right then, let me see what you have."

After a couple of hours, Bobby got in his car as he waited for Xavier to answer his call.

"Xavier Bailey's office."

"Hey, Linda, it's Bobby Johnson. Can you connect me with Xavier again, please?"

"Hello, Bobby, you have perfect timing. He actually just got back from another meeting. One moment please."

"Bobby Johnson, I was just about to call you and tell you about the endorsement deal I just secured for you."

"Wow, that's great, my first endorsement!" Bobby said with a smile so big you could see it through the phone.

"I told you we had big plans for you, superstar. This is just the beginning!"

"How much am I getting paid, and what am I endorsing?"

"I apologize for rushing, Bobby, but I'm late for another meeting. I will transfer the money to your account, and fill you in with all the details later."

"No problem, X, just keep those endorsement deals coming. Hey, I just need one more favor."

"Sure, what's up?"

"Well, instead of twenty thousand dollars, I need you to give me forty-two thousand. Is that possible on such short notice?"

After a brief pause, Xavier responded,

"Yeah, sure, that's no problem. Just come down in a couple of hours, and Linda will have the paperwork ready for you to sign."

"You're the best, Xavier!"

"I know, remember? That's why you hired me! Tell all your team-mates about me too! See you later."

Bobby was filled with relief as he hung the phone up. His pride and competitiveness almost wrote a check he could not cash. He'd gotten into a bidding war with another rookie on the team for a diamond-studded watch that drew the attention of all of his teammates that were in the locker room.

Never being one to ever back down from a good challenge, Bobby refused to lose, especially to another rookie. With every bid the cheers grew louder and louder, until Bobby finally prevailed. In his mind, he earned the respect from everybody in the locker room.

"Good job, rook; you balled out!" Derek stated.

Yes, he thought to himself, *I did!*

"Like my grandfather told me growing up; happy wife, happy life." –Bobby

A week later, after the surprising upset of Miami, the best team in the league, on their own home court, thanks to Bobby's last-second three-pointer, the locker room was rocking with excitement as if they had just won the championship.

"Woo, we did it! Nice shot, rook!" screamed one teammate. After giving a slew of interviews, the celebration continued as Bobby entered the restaurant on South Beach with his teammates for dinner.

"Did you see everyone's faces when Bobby hit that three to win the game?" Greg asked.

"Yeah, it caught everyone in the arena off guard because we were only down by one. No one expected the rookie to let it fly from deep!"

Sitting quietly, with his chest poked out as he beamed with pride listening to everyone discuss his heroics, he suddenly heard the sound of a familiar voice coming from behind him.

"Great game, Bobby Johnson. I am so proud of you!"

It was not hard to tell what his teammates were thinking from the looks they had on their faces.

He smiled as he stood to turn around, setting his eyes on perfection times two.

"Thanks, baby girl!" Bobby responded, as he bent down to kiss his wife.

"Everyone, let me introduce you to my motivation. This is my wife, Nicola, and her sister, Tabitha."

Bobby's wife Nicola smiled and said,

"Hello everyone! It's great to finally meet the guys keeping my husband from coming home to me."

The table erupted with laughter as Derek yelled out in a distorted voice, "He's a damn fool!"

After a few minutes passed, Bobby looked at his wife and asked, "So, how'd it go?"

With a smile on her face she responded,

"We got her! After a few hours of going back and forth, she finally agreed to join our team."

"That's great news, baby. Let's toast to your success!"

"You know, I have to take a rain check on that, because we actually should be leaving now. We are meeting in about an hour to finalize the contract."

"Well, congrats, honey. You are on the fast track to becoming that mogul after all!"

"No, Bobby, we are a team. I could not have done it without you."

"I love you, baby. See you back at the hotel."

"Ok, love you too, baby girl. Call if you need anything."

As Bobby turned to sit back down, Greg asked, "What was all that about?"

Beaming with pride, Bobby answered,

"My wife is starting a clothing line, and just hired the best designer money can buy!"

Derek chimed in, "That's impressive. While all of our women's focus is on spending our money, yours is focused on *making* money. And she's drop-dead gorgeous, too. She's definitely a keeper! Can she sing? I'm thinking about starting a record label," he added, as the table started laughing.

"Yeah, she's supported me through all the moves I had to make playing in Europe as I pursued my dream of becoming an NBA basketball player, and never once complained. The least I could do to show my appreciation is to invest in her endeavor. Like my grandfather always told me growing up; happy wife, happy life."

"Well amen to that!" Greg responded. "That's so sweet, you better stop 'cause you are moving me to tears, dawg!"

The table again erupted with laughter at that statement, while Derek instructed the waitress to hand Bobby the check.

"Since you are so good at underwriting, go ahead and take care of this, rook. We'll see you back at the hotel," Derek said, as they all got up to leave.

Bobby frowned as he watched his teammates leave, finally realizing he has to pay the seven thousand dollar bill himself. As he sat and waited for the waitress to return with his credit card, he reflected on the lie he just told his teammates.

Nicola hated everything about living abroad, and she never hesitated to let Bobby know how she felt. Nicola always guilted him into buying her expensive clothes, purses, and other items, even though he could not afford it.

She could not understand why they struggled to make ends meet, but Bobby still found a way to bail his family out of whatever jam they found themselves in when they called for help. The only thing that had saved their marriage to this point was his recent NBA contract.

Committed to reflecting the perfect life, Bobby made sure no one knew the financial drama he faced daily being married to Nicola.

She's a keeper, Bobby said to himself as he shook his head. *If they only knew!*

"From now on, only call me on my cell phone." –Xavier

Bobby was cooking breakfast when suddenly he heard his phone ring. From the ringtone he knew it was Xavier. He ran to answer the phone, but it stopped ringing before he got there. After Bobby finished cooking breakfast, he picked his phone back up to see if Xavier had left a message.

"Hey, superstar. I need for you to cancel your plans for this afternoon, and meet me at our normal meeting spot. I have a proposition for you!"

It must be very important, Bobby thought to himself before texting Xavier to confirm his attendance. *The last time Xavier called me sounding like this, it changed my life!* he thought, as he flashed back to that moment that brought him here.

Bobby was an unhappy ballplayer in the middle of his third season in Europe, playing on his fifth team. Feeling like his agent at the time was not delivering on the promises that convinced Bobby to hire him in the first place, Bobby became disgruntled about his dim future.

During a random conversation on Facebook with one of his former AAU coaches, Bobby expressed his displeasure with his current situation. As fate would have it, while scouting players for his agency, Xavier bumped into the old coach. During that brief encounter, Xavier asked how Bobby was doing. That is when the coach explained the dire circumstances his old star player found himself dealing with.

Excited about the news he'd just received, Xavier immediately reached out to Bobby and was able to convince him after a short conversation to sign with him. However, that was easier said than done.

Bobby was projected to be a late first-round pick coming out of college, and because of that, his agent gave him a line of credit to live off of until he started getting paid. Instead of frugally using the line of credit, he instantly felt the pressure of living like a millionaire, even though the draft was still a few months away. Instead of staying on campus in the dorm, Bobby leased a plush, furnished apartment in the heart of the city. He also bought a cherry-red Mercedes Benz, and attended various developmental camps to prepare himself for the next level. All paid with the credit line.

To everyone's surprise, Bobby did not get drafted at all. He tried out for a number of teams, but could not land a spot. With no other options to choose from, Bobby made the tough decision to take his talents to the south of France to play for a B-level team, making B-level money.

Not thoroughly reading through the contract he'd signed with his agent, Bobby was unaware that he had agreed to a five-year contract. If he fired his agent before the agreed-upon term, the money that Bobby used from the line would be reclassified as a short- term loan payable within 30 days of cancellation. So Bobby was trapped in a lose-lose situation; that is, until Xavier came along.

Even though it seemed like a hard pill to swallow, firing his agent with no guarantees that his situation would improve, it turned out to be the best decision Bobby ever made, because within two weeks not only did Xavier pay the remaining balance of $250,000, freeing Bobby, but he also got Bobby a tryout and signed to a team in the NBA. And for that he developed total loyalty to Xavier.

"Hey, Bobby, sorry I'm late. My last meeting ran over."

"No problem, Xavier; what's going on?"

"Wow, no small talk from you, huh?"

Laughing, Bobby responded, "No, it's not that at all. I'm just interested to find out what's so pressing that I had to clear my schedule!"

"Is it another endorsement deal or something?"

"It's something like that?"

With his adrenaline running and interest piqued to the fullest, Bobby demanded with excitement.

"Enough already with the dramatics, cut to the chase!"

"Okay, okay," he responded, as he took a sip from his glass. "I'm starting a new firm that not only deals with contract negotiations, but also investing options for athletes and entertainers. And I not only want you to be the face of the firm, but part owner as well."

"Sounds very intriguing, but I know only what you tell me about investing. What do I have to do?"

"It's simple. Just connect me with the guys you've met throughout the league, and I'll take care of the rest!"

Taking out his cell phone and scrolling through his list of contacts, Bobby replied,

"That's easy enough. Here are a couple of guys now that I know would be interested."

Happy about the outcome of the meeting, Xavier smiled and said,

"From now on, only call me on my cell phone. I don't want anyone in the office to catch wind of our partnership. You're about to make money hand over fist, young man. Enjoy the ride!"

"I'm sure she'd rather me spend my money on a bunch of guys than a bunch of women."
–Bobby

"Wake up, Bobby and explain why you have a bill for 10 cell phones. Are you cheating on me?"

Shaken from being jarred out of his sleep, all Bobby could form his lips to say was,

"Huh?"

"I opened your cell phone bill, and it shows that you are paying for 10 phones. Explain yourself!"

"Oh, that. It's the fellas' I'm paying for."

"What fellas? The guys that follow you around like kids hoping for a piece of candy? You only knew two of them before this year, and now you are financing their lifestyles? Are you kidding me? We finally get your family out of your pockets, only for you to let guys who you could not depend on to help you out of a jam if you needed them to, in?"

"Nicola!" Bobby screamed, before being cut off.

"Fix it now!" She yelled as she left, slamming the door.

Bobby thought to himself,

If she acted like that over some inexpensive cell phone plans, she would really lose it if she found out I am paying rent on six apartments for them to share.

Bobby always thought growing up that the best trait his grandfather had was the willingness to help those in need. Through the years, Bobby had developed that same trait. He had always been a sucker for a hard luck story, and now that he was finally in the NBA, making more money than he had ever made before, and he had no personal finance skills, he was ripe for the picking.

Yes, every time they do anything as a group, from shopping to dining, from clubbing to traveling, Bobby paid.

But in his mind, God gave him the ability and opportunity to earn a great living. It would be blasphemy not to share the wealth.

"She'll get over it," he thought out loud. "I'm sure she'd rather me spend my money on a bunch of guys than a bunch of women!" he rationalized as he lay back down in bed, thinking, *Whatever!*

"You are in the NBA now, making a hell of a lot more money!" –Cherie

For as far back as he could remember, Bobby was not the typical athlete that always hung out in cliques with other jocks. He always considered himself a man of the people, and that was where he found himself today, amongst the regular people, working out at the neighborhood gym.

Sure, people recognized who he was, and on occasion they would try to get his attention for various reasons. But, with loud music blaring through his headphones, Bobby was able to block everything and everyone out as he got on the treadmill to complete his workout session.

Bobby unplugged his headphones from his iPod and connected them to the treadmill to watch the last few minutes of ESPN. After a couple of minutes of routine stories of the previous night's games, Bobby read something that caused him to feel like he got caught with a right hook to the jaw, becoming so lightheaded he missed a step and stumbled off the treadmill.

Embarrassed at the thought of someone witnessing what just happened, he tried his best to play like nothing happened. Bobby gathered himself and rushed to the locker room to retrieve his gym bag.

He rushed to his car and immediately logged on to espn.com to see if in fact he had read what he thought he'd read. To his dismay, his eyes were not deceiving him, because in bold print the leading story title read: BOBBY JOHNSON DEADBEAT DAD!!

"What are they talking about?" Bobby asked himself, as he picked up the phone and dialed.

"Hello," the voice answered on the other end.

"Yeah, Cherie, it's me, Bobby. What the hell is going on?"

"What do you mean what's going on?"

"I take good care of my son, and now they are reporting in the media that I don't! Did they get that from you?"

"All I did was go down to the child support office to request a modification hearing. I guess when I told them who my son's father was and explained to them the situation, they decided to report the story."

Angry at what he'd just heard, Bobby screamed through the phone,

"But we had an agreement! If you wanted more money, all you had to do was call!"

"I called on three different occasions and spoke with your loving wife each time about the situation. She would end the conversation the same way every time, stating that you were unavailable, but she would relay the message to you."

"Okay," Bobby responded. "Why couldn't you just wait until you spoke with me? Do you understand the potential harm this bad press could cause me?"

Cherie, cool and calm, responded,

"My obligation is not to protect you, it is to take care of our son the best that I can. The agreement we made was more than three years ago, when you first went overseas, and it was based on the money you were making then. You are in the NBA now, making a hell of a lot more money."

"How do you know what I'm making?"

"Because I see you every day on television with your fancy clothes and expensive jewelry. Plus, my mother forwarded me a link to a website that did a story about you flying on private jets hosting poker games. I could send you the link if you want!" Cherie stated sarcastically, as she continued.

"While you are out pissing your money away living life to the full-est, not once have you offered to increase what you pay me for our son. I've done my job, now do yours. See you in court!" she screamed, before hanging up the phone.

Concerned more about his image in the public eye of being labeled a deadbeat dad than the potential increase in child support, Bobby dialed the number to the only person that could help him with this situation.

The line picked up and before he could say anything, Xavier said,

"Hey, superstar. I've been expecting your call."

"This mess is driving me crazy. What are my options?"

"You have no other options but to pay her."

"The bad press can adversely affect your chances of getting any future endorsement deals. And remember, you are a business owner now, in an industry where reputation is everything. Give me Cherie's number, and I'll work everything out."

Relieved at what Xavier just told him, Bobby gave him the number.

"Okay, I'll work on this now. Don't watch television for the next few days. I will call you when it's done. Go get some rest; you sound tired!"

"Okay, I will. Thanks, X, I owe you my life. It's scary where I'd be without you."

"Don't be so hard on yourself, Bobby. We all make mistakes."

Mentally drained from the situation, Bobby hung up the phone and headed home as Xavier suggested.

"Why didn't Nicola tell me Cherie called?" he asked himself.

As he pulled into the driveway he noticed his wife's car parked outside with the doors and trunk open.

"Great, I will get to the bottom of this right now!"

Bobby turned the knob to the front door and walked into the house. He had a curious look on his face when he heard the sound of zippers being zipped up in the guest room. As he entered the room and made eye contact with his wife, she screamed as loudly as she could,

"The checks bounced, Bobby!"

With a look of confusion on his face from the news he'd just received he asked,

"What are you talking about? What checks?"

"Don't play dumb with me! You know, the checks I used to pay for the designer's fees and for the materials she needed."

"She is now requesting that I pay her only in cash to avoid any future hiccups. How embarrassed do you think I felt when she expressed sympathy for my situation, like I was some kind of charity case needing a hand out?"

She headed toward Bobby and screamed,

"Move out of my way!"

"Where are you going?" Bobby asked, as he stepped aside.

"Don't worry about it!" she replied.

He followed his wife down the hall towards the master bedroom. She was furious. He had seen her angry before, but never quite like this. He found himself amazed at how a woman so short and petite could render in him so much damage.

"My sister was right! I put my future on hold for you and followed your ass around the world! All I ever got in return from you is trouble!"

Nicola made the fast turn into the bedroom, where she'd already laid out her luggage. She began rifling through her closet and came out with large swaths of dresses and slacks braced in her tiny arms. She stuffed them unceremoniously into the large suitcase, then she returned for more.

"You've been operating in the red since you signed that NBA contract, because you live your life like there is no tomorrow. There are people in the stands cheering for you and worshipping you like you are some god, who are working regular 9 to 5 jobs, and they have more money in the bank than you! You make all this money, and still live paycheck to paycheck. This is just the midway point of your first year in the league, and you've already accumulated how much debt? Imagine what you will accumulate if you keep this pace up after year two, if there is a year two. You are what they call the working poor. And now you have this baby mama drama creeping up. Bobby, I've had enough. It's not worth it, I want a divorce!"

Furious from the bomb Nicola just dropped on him, Bobby responded,

"Divorce what? It's your fault! This all could have been avoided if you had just told me Cherie called!"

"My fault?" Nicola asked with a puzzled look on her face before continuing,

"You see? That's what I'm talking about. Just like you told me your mom used to do; you take no ownership when it comes to issues in your life. You knew what you were getting into when you laid down with her. Stop resorting to the lost little boy act and man up. Your granddad can't help you out of this situation. Bye!" she said, as she grabbed her suitcases and ran out the door.

Not wanting his wife to see the affects her rampage left on him, Bobby slammed the door behind her. Truly shaken, he ran to the window and watched her drive away. As she disappeared from sight he stood there, shaking his head and looked up, asking,

"What next?"

"We can't afford to take care of them." –Fran

Bobby arrived late to the arena and sat on the sidelines, watching, as his team prepared to face Miami for the first time since his game-winning shot, without him. It will be the third game in row he has missed due to an illness that popped up all of a sudden that he can't seem to shake.

The doctors have run numerous tests, but still can't determine what is ailing him, causing Bobby's coaches and even a couple of his teammates to question his toughness.

"Johnson."

"Yeah, what's up, Mike?"

"Mr. Gordon wants to see you in his office."

"Really?" he asked. "Me?"

What does Mr. Gordon want to see me for? Am I getting cut? he thought to himself.

As he nervously walked off the sidelines towards the general manager's office, Bobby felt every sympathetic eye on the court staring at him as if they knew what was going on. He had an eerie feeling that did not sit well with him. As he approached the door to Mr. Gordon's office, he thought to himself, *Let's get it over with!* as he pushed the door open.

"Good morning, Mr. Gordon. You wanted to see me?"

"Yes, Bobby. I want to offer my condolences."

"Condolences, for what?"

Surprised at Bobby's response, Mr. Gordon stated,

"Oh, you haven't heard yet?"

"Heard what?"

"We received the call this morning. We tried calling you, but you did not answer. So we asked a couple of your teammates to reach out to you, and assumed they were able to get hold of you."

At this point Bobby had no clue what to prepare himself for, but from the look on his general manager's face, he could tell that it was not good.

"That's all right, just tell me! What is it?"

"Your grandparents need you to call them immediately. It's about your sister. Bobby, I'm sorry to have to tell you, but she passed away last night."

"She what?" Bobby asked, with pain in his voice.

"I'm sorry, son. The team will support you through this trying time. Take as much time off as you need."

"Thank you, Mr. Gordon. I will let you know something as soon as I find out what's going on."

Bobby raced out of the arena and called his grandparents from the car. As expected, the pain in his grandmother's voice when she answered was unbearable.

"She's gone, baby, she's gone. And your mother and brother are already here, rummaging through her things. Cindy has nothing for

118 | Bruce Wayne

them. She didn't even leave anything for her two babies. We can't afford to take care of them. We don't even have enough to pay for her burial!"

"What happened?"

"She's been battling cancer."

"What? Why didn't anyone tell me?"

"Enough, please!"

Realizing that it was not all about him and his feelings, and understanding how distraught his grandmother was of Cindy's passing, he eased up on the line of questioning. With tears in his eyes he said,

"I'm on my way. Don't worry about a thing, Grandma. I'll take care of everything when I get there."

"Cindy didn't belong to a church she could ask help from?" –Melanie

"Why don't you just sell Cindy's car, Gram? I'm sure the proceeds would easily be enough to cover the cost of her funeral," Andrew suggested.

"That is not an option, Andrew," their grandmother responded.

Surprised by her answer, Andrew asked why.

"Cindy had taken out a title loan using her car as collateral to help her make ends meet. She became delinquent on the loan, and they picked the car up while she was in the hospital and have already sold it."

"Are you kidding me?" Andrew responded in disbelief, before being cut off by his mother.

"Cindy didn't belong to a church that she could've asked for help from?"

Shaking her head no, Grandmother responded, "We reached out to Jacob, but still have not heard anything from him. And the children's father has no room for them in his life with his new family. So we are forced to take care of them. Granddad and I can't do this by ourselves. We are begging you all to pitch in so we can give Cindy the sending off she deserves."

"I can't commit to anything, Mom. I have to ask Randal," Melanie responded.

"The kids' father has always been absent from their lives, so it does not surprise me that he wants nothing to do with them. And you're definitely not going to hear from that punk Jacob.

"Andrew, that is not necessary!" Fran responded in disgust.

"Well, what I'm trying to say is, with Cindy gone, his well has run dry!"

As Andrew turned to face Bobby, he asked,

"Why doesn't the rich basketball player step up?"

Overwhelmed with the sad realization that he would never see his sister again, Bobby responded in a low, soft voice as he took out his credit card.

"I'll pay for everything, Grams."

His grandmother's face lit up as she took his credit card from him.

"Thank you, baby. I'll be right back," she stated, as she turned and walked into the funeral home's business office.

"Be careful, Mom, lighting is about to strike!" Andrew stated in a negative tone.

"What's that supposed to mean?" Bobby asked.

"The fact that you are finally thinking about someone other than yourself, and paying for Cindy's funeral."

"What are you talking about? Ever since I went overseas, I've been bailing every one of you out of shit that you got yourself into. I don't even know where to begin to tell you what I've lost because of that!"

"Bobby?"

"Yes, Mom?"

"Everything you did for us you were supposed to do, as repayment for what we sacrificed when you were younger, with all the camps you attended and the equipment you got."

"You would not have made it to the level you've made it to if we all did not play our part."

"Remember, family takes care of family, at any cost!"

Furious at his mother and brother's attempt to make him feel guilty for cutting them off, Bobby attempted to give them a piece of his mind before being interrupted by the office door opening.

As his grandmother approached him, Bobby could tell by the look of disappointment on her face that something wasn't right.

"Is everything okay, Gram?" he asked.

"No, honey, not at all."

"What's wrong?"

"Your credit card was declined."

"What? That's impossible; it's a Black card!"

In a defeated tone, his grandmother responded,

"We tried running it through three or four times, and it was declined every time, so I just went ahead and paid for everything with the little bit of money Granddad and I had ."

He didn't know what was worse; the embarrassment of his credit card being rejected and his grandparents having to pay for something he couldn't, or the fact that it happened in front of his brother, who stood behind his mother with a snide smirk on his face.

"I apologize, Grams. I'll call my agent and get to the bottom of this right now."

"Where are you, Xavier, and what the hell did you do with all of my money?" –Bobby

It had been eight days since Cindy's home going, and Bobby was still an emotional wreck; but not just because he'd lost his sister. He couldn't seem to find Xavier, and had left numerous messages on his cell phone.

Bobby had called almost every hour on the hour since that embarrassing moment in front of his family at the funeral home. After a couple more days went by, and still no sign of Xavier, Bobby decided to go against Xavier's request and call him at the office. To his surprise, the line was disconnected.

"What the hell is going on?" he asked himself.

Returning to the team for the first time in almost two weeks, Bobby decided to leave a little earlier than usual so he could go by the bank to check on his accounts. Because it was usually Xavier, his missing agent, handling his banking accounts, Bobby felt like a fish out of water when he entered the large financial establishment and walked towards the young man standing at the desk.

"Excuse me; I need to speak with a representative to check on my accounts."

"My pleasure, sir. I can help you with that."

"Do you have your debit card with you so I can pull up your accounts?"

"No, but I have my driver's license. Will that be sufficient?"

"Yes, that should be fine," the banker answered, as he reached for Bobby's license.

After typing in a few commands on the computer and verifying Bobby's identity, the young banker said,

"Mr. Johnson, I appreciate your patience. The system shows that you are a private wealth client, so I have to refer you to one of my colleagues in that department. One moment please."

Agitated that he had to wait longer, Bobby just nodded at the message the banker just delivered.

Shortly after leaving, the young banker returned and announced to Bobby that not only did he find a wealth manager to help him, but the actual wealth manager assigned to him.

"He will be out in a few, Mr. Johnson."

"Thank you."

After a few minutes, Bobby heard a voice coming from behind him.

"Mr. Johnson, I apologize for keeping you waiting. It's my pleasure to finally meet you. I just got through speaking with Xavier. Is everything okay?"

Surprised at the comment the banker just made about just speaking with Xavier, Bobby decided to play it cool and responded,

"Yeah, everything is fine. I just want to find out what I have in my accounts."

"No problem, Mr. Johnson. Just follow me to my cubicle, and we'll get that information for you immediately."

As Bobby got up to follow the banker he nervously wondered to himself,

Is Xavier avoiding me?

After meeting with the banker, Bobby walked out of the bank in such a way that a blind man could see that something was wrong. He picked up his phone in a last-ditch effort to get in touch with Xavier. He got excited when the line finally picked up. However, it was not Xavier's voice Bobby heard coming from the other end. It was the automated voice letting everyone know that Xavier's message mailbox was full, and to try again later.

Slamming his phone down on the floor of his car, Bobby screamed,

"Where are you Xavier, and what the hell did you do with all of my money?"

While looking through his account history with the banker, Bobby was given a hard dose of reality that shook him to the core.

His account had just been overdrawn by more than thirty thousand dollars. Gone was the signing bonus money Xavier claimed he put in his account, gone was the endorsement deal money. The only thing he had showing positive was a CD for a measly five thousand dollars.

Finally making it to the arena, Bobby got out of the car to head inside.

"Welcome back, rook!" he heard, as he entered the locker room.

"Thanks, it's good to be back. I need to get to work, he answered.

After getting dressed in his practice gear, he gave himself a self-talk while he made the short journey to the practice area.

"I will let karma take care of Xavier. I refuse to let anybody know about this. I will not be the laughing stock of the entire league!"

A few weeks later, as the playoffs approached, Bobby ran down the court in the second half of the most important game of the year.

Wow, she really is divorcing me. My sister is gone, I'm losing my house, my child support payments have been increased by almost 250%, and I have no

money! Bobby thought before being snapped out of his trance by the sound of a whistle.

"Travel #10!" the referee called.

Bobby's coach's voice could be heard screaming over the chorus of boos.

"Run the damn play, Johnson! What the hell are you doing out there?"

That question had been asked of him so often over the past few weeks that Bobby had lost count.

It's not due to his lack of trying. He was just so distracted about his personal life, caused by his dire financial situation, that 'he couldn't think straight. Over the last three games, Bobby had seen his playing time dwindle due to his low production. He was feeling the heat from everyone associated with the team, from the ball boy to the general manager.

I need to hit this shot! he thought, as he shot the ball.

With every brick and air ball he shot, the moans and groans from the crowd grew louder and louder, until finally he hit a three-pointer to tie the game. The crowd erupted with an emphatic roar as the referee signaled for a timeout.

While the teams exited the court, the team doctors could be seen running towards a figure rolling in pain on the court.

"Who is that?" a fan asked.

When the bodies around him cleared, another fan answered, "It's Bobby Johnson."

"Damn, that's crazy!" –Bobby

A couple of long, agonizing years later, Bobby sat penniless in his car doing what he has done over and over again, reflecting on what was. In just a few short months he went from the highest of the highs, achieving his lifelong goal of playing in the NBA, to the lowest of the lows, suffering a career-ending injury from a torn ACL and broken femur, all on the same play.

His meteoric rise to perceived stardom gave him a false sense of security that led him to live a reckless life when it came to his personal financial management. Spending money like it was never going to stop coming in. *Where did I go wrong?* used to be the question he asked himself repeatedly, but because of so much time to himself to figure it out, he now knows.

He finally found out what happened to Xavier when he got a call from the authorities to testify against him for financial crimes he committed against a slew of other players in the league, including Greg, the teammate Xavier wanted Bobby to steer clear from, obviously in an attempt to avoid Greg from exposing his shady business dealings with him.

I got off so easy that I didn't appreciate it, Bobby thought to himself about the financial problems he had when he played in Europe that Xavier bailed him out of.

"I should have learned from my mother and the bullshit she's gone through with Randall, what happens when you put yourself in a position where you need someone, or depend solely on that person, sacrificing your better judgment!"

"Why didn't I just count my blessings and been satisfied about my second chance?" he said aloud, while looking in the mirror at his reflection and shaking his head in disgust.

"I have allowed my competitive nature in, refusing to let anyone out do me. Now I sit here without two nickels to rub together or a pot to piss in!"

"I didn't need that huge house and all those cars; it was just me and Nicola. That was all for show."

"Shit, I guess the one with the most toys don't win, they just have more bills!" He thought, as he took a deep breath.

"I should've never been so trusting when it came to other people handling the money I made.

"Xavier did to me what I allowed him to do.

"Deep down inside I knew that it was wrong for me to stretch my finances so far past the limit that checks bounced, all in an effort to fund a business venture that was doomed from the start. Nicola didn't have the savvy or sense to run a successful business. I should've passed on appeasing her demands and throwing the money away that I did on that crap.

"I should've gotten the agreement I made with Cherie pertaining to the child support in writing and increased it when I signed the new contract, to avoid any issues.

"And even though I hate to admit it, Nicola was correct. What man in his right mind financially supports a bunch of other grown and able-bodied men, especially ones they barely know?

"I wanted so much to be different from my family, but I see now what they mean when they say you're cut from the same cloth!

"Life is wild!" he thought to himself.

"Here I sit, in my grandparents' driveway, with no options to make a living and worse yet, no savings to sustain me until I can figure some things out!"

As he finished his thought, he was distracted by a knock on the car window.

"Hey, Uncle Bobby, welcome back. Grandma just had us clean up your old room for you!"

"Okay, little man, I appreciate it. Run and tell Gram that I'll be in, in a few minutes."

"Okay. I am so happy you are here!"

"Me too! Now go let her know so she won't get worried!"

"Okay, Uncle Bobby!"

As he watched his nephew turn and run with excitement to announce his arrival, Bobby turned his attention back on the man in the mirror and said out loud,

"After all the money I've made over the last few years playing professional basketball, who would've thought that when it was all over I would have to move back in with my grandparents?"

"Damn…. That's crazy!"

Fran

"I'm sorry, baby!"
–Fran

With her squabbling daughter and grandsons having finally taken their arguments to the hallway, Fran gazed down at her sleeping husband. She tried to remember the good times, but found she could only concentrate on the bad. She felt wracked with guilt and sorrow at what appears to have been William's failed attempt at suicide.

"I'm sorry, baby!" she cried, as William lay motionless.

"When you told me you were going to kill yourself, I just thought you were looking for sympathy from me by trying to assume the role of the victim."

Fran had stood by William's side through thick and thin, so she knew very well how their finances had gotten so ugly that her husband would be crying even as he laughed. But she could have never anticipated this.

A tear formed in her eye as William drew a labored breath, then let it out as if it caused him great relief. Every intake appeared to be a struggle, every exhale a joy. It reminded her of the twin nature of the way they had cared for their daughter and grandchildren. There was always the joy in helping, and often the joy in literally taking them in. As she reflected on the joy it brought them, she quickly realized the cost each joy came with; a cost that now seemed beyond measure.

"Don't worry; they are just committed to making this situation harder than it should be!" –Melanie

Fran recalled the day Melanie arrived with her young children in tow. She had expected her grandchildren to be upset, but not this upset. Little Cindy exited the car, with her vision blurred from all the crying she had been doing during the long trip. Her face was still full of tears, even as her mother helped her carry her luggage from the car. Andrew only had scowls for everyone he faced, including his grandfather, who had always been his right hand man at every family gathering. But as it turned out, Bobby employed an even more devastating manner to express his anger. His determined silence spoke volumes about how he felt at having to pack up all his belongings, leave his teammates, and move to North Carolina to live with his grandparents. The pure sight was heart-breaking to Fran, who had been so excited to accept her daughter and grandchildren back in her arms and home. But all that excitement evaporated the moment she laid eyes on her granddaughter's face. Feeling guilty, her lips quivered as she watched the young children struggle to lug their giant suitcases toward the ranch-style home that Fran and William had recently downsized to.

Seeing the sad look on her parents' faces, Melanie said,

"Don't worry, they are just committed to making this situation harder than it should be. Once they meet new friends, everything will be fine," she explained, as she kissed her father and mother on the cheek. Fran nodded in understanding, but not with any measure of reassurance. She had so wanted this unexpected reunion to bring the family together. But even now, it seemed clear that it would only drive them apart. She loved and disliked her daughter all at once in that moment. Loved her for the wonderful children she had raised, and for her valiant efforts at attempting to provide a nice life for them, even after her husband was carted away to prison. She disliked her for all the financial mistakes and lack of work ethic she had that forced everyone to adjust their lives by having to make this ugly choice.

Of course, over the months and years that would follow, Fran would do everything in her power to make her daughter and grandchildren welcomed and well-cared for, but it seemed to her that from the first day forward, the relationship was never the same. Poor financial decisions had crippled her daughter, and now they had come to form a kind of debilitating disease on the entire family.

As she continued to reflect on what had happened, Fran's mind fast-forwarded in time to a more recent memory that caused pain and sorrow.

**"Your grandmother and I wanted to come personally
and thank you for ruining our lives!" –William**

"Do you know what this is, son?" William asked.

It was an unseasonably warm day, as Fran recalled it, the kind of sweltering heat that forces everyone inside, making the city look more like a ghost town. In this way, it felt to Fran like she, William, and their eldest grandson Andrew were the only people in the world standing under the radiating sun.

Andrew looked away from the paper William held out to him. His expression suggested that he knew very well what the paper meant, but said nothing. In the grandson in whom she'd had such pride, Fran for the first time felt the insidious emotions of pity and distaste. Andrew had always shown such promise. If ever there was a man who possessed William's drive and potential to provide for his family, it was Andrew. But here he had been caught in a lie so deep that it threatened to destroy his future. His girlfriend Corrine had already left him because of all the trouble he found himself in. And even as Fran and William stood at the end of his driveway, Andrew had begun the process of moving all of his boxes out of his house after finally being evicted. The sheer number of flat screen televisions that lined the lawn lent the scene an element of unreal. The TVs made Fran feel a little like she had wandered into an outdoor sports bar after hours. She hated every television for what it represented. It was just another example of Andrew's lack of perspective in life. How it had come to this, she could not be certain. All she knew was that she did not like what she and her husband had come to do.

"It's a letter, letting me know that I'm being sued by the finance company," William announced, holding the slip of paper out further, as if to urge Andrew to take it.

Finally complying with his grandfather's gesture, Andrew snatched the paper out of William's hand and held it at his side, without even giving it a single glance.

"Do you know why they are suing me, Andrew?" William asked.

Andrew shrugged, without saying a word.

Fran began to cry.

"Because of your irresponsible decision to cancel the auto insurance on the Benz you bamboozled me into financing for you. Your selfish course of action left me totally exposed, and now I am responsible for paying the whole amount back."

Andrew's face grew bloodshot red. For a moment, Fran could not tell whether he would start to cry, or he was about to scream. He steeled himself up as if to do the latter, but when he opened his mouth, nothing followed. His eyes began to water, his limbs began to quake. To his credit, he held back the sobs.

William continued his tongue-lashing.

"Your grandmother and I wanted to come and thank you personally for ruining our lives!"

Finally having enough of being drilled by his grandfather, Andrew's anger reached a boiling point, causing him to disrespectfully bark back at William.

"Ruined your life? Whatever, dude. I'm the one facing prison time. I can't worry about your problems, because mine are much bigger!"

"You're facing prison time because of your own action–"

Before William could finish the statement, Andrew stormed off, waving his arms dismissively, which was an act Fran had seen many times since her grandson was just a boy.

"Please just nod if you have the money you owe us." –Fran

Shaking her head as her mind came back to present time, she turned as William struggled to roll onto his side. Fran tried to call out to him, but he remained under the haze of the drugs. The sight reminded her of the time she visited her granddaughter Cindy when she was in a similar state. Her beautiful granddaughter was stricken with cancer at a young age, and she lay in the bed in the observation room following her final and ultimately deadly round of radiation therapy. The hospital bills by this time had become a substantial burden for Cindy, so it was with a heavy heart that Fran visited the observation room to do the most difficult thing she had ever had to do.

With the guilt gripping her throat, making it hard to speak, Fran asked,

"How are you feeling, honey?"

Cindy gave her sad grandmother a weak nod as she struggled to smile. Fran could not ever recall a person looking sicker.

"I'm sorry to have to ask you this," Fran said, with a tear sliding down her cheek.

"But today's the deadline,"

"Gram, I–"

"No, don't talk," Fran interrupted.

"You need to keep your strength. Please just nod if you have the money you owe us."

The guilt began to overwhelm Fran, causing her to start sobbing uncontrollably.

"I know you're a single mother and you are battling this horrible thing, but your grandfather and I are completely wiped out. We're out of options. At this rate, we will lose what little things we still have."

With her skin turning a green hue, Cindy drew a long, labored breath as she lowered her bed all the way down and said nothing as she looked up at the ceiling.

"Just nod if you have the money," Fran pleaded.

Cindy merely stared.

"Please tell me something, honey," Fran begged, as the tears from her eyes flowed more rapidly.

Cindy closed her eyes and turned her head away.

Even now, Fran could hardly breathe as she recalled the memory of her last meeting with Cindy, where she found herself asking for money from her dying granddaughter. The fallout had been nearly as painful, as well. Cindy died without leaving a will or any type of guardianship plan. Initially, knowing the children's biological father couldn't care less about taking them in, and factoring in the possible social security money that would come to the kids, Melanie and Andrew argued about who would be the best guardian for the kids. However, after discovering that there was no windfall coming the childrens' way, they declined to offer them a place to live, ultimately forcing their grandparents' hand in opening their home to the youngest generation of the family. The thought made Fran sick.

She laid her hand on her husband's shoulder, trying to caress away the guilt and pain, but her mind kept flashing back to things she would rather forget. The next vision that came to her mind was that of her husband and youngest grandson, Bobby, struggling together to remove the foreclosure sign the bank had hammered into the front yard. William was well aware of the illegality of his actions, but no one living in the tiny home could bear the embarrassment any longer. Their house was only a few thousand dollars away from being paid completely off, but Andrew came to them with an issue he needed help with, so they refinanced the mortgage to help him out.

After a couple of payments, Andrew stopped paying them back, and when William was forced to retire, he fell behind on the payments enough to lose the house. Never repaying them for Cindy's funeral like he had promised, and forced to move back into his grandparents' home after his sudden fall from grace, Bobby felt the least he could do · to start paying them back for all he and his family had wrought over the years was to help remove the sign.

Bobby looked thicker on that day than Fran had ever seen him. He often spoke about his plans to go see a specialist that could help him with his injury, in an attempt to return to the game he loved and unfortunately, the only way he knew how to make money. However, Fran never saw much of an effort from Bobby. Her grandson had become an emotional wreck since losing his wife, along with the life he had grown so quickly accustomed to. He spent most of his days sitting on his grandparents' couch that also served as his nightly bed, staring at the television, watching repeats on ESPN. It always made Fran sick to her stomach when she returned home after a long day of job hunting to find Bobby right where she had left him at dawn, but nothing could make her sicker than the sight of two of her favorite men in life looking like two whipped dogs as they dragged the foreclosure sign into the empty garage.

Fran never told her husband this, but she had taken the bus to the homeless shelter downtown, wanting to scout out what their near future would bring. As she stared at the hopeless souls lining the halls of that horrible place, she could not help but wonder what their stories were, and how her family had sunk so low. She could not picture William in the soup line. She could not picture her grandchildren sleeping on dirty, soiled cots. She could not imagine having to panhandle for cash in the streets. That is, until now, unless something miraculous happened, and soon.

Fran got up and went to the sink in William's room to wash the dried-up tears from her face. When she looked up to grab a towel to dry her hands, she stopped when she saw her reflection looking back at her.

"Who am I fooling?" she asked the reflection in the mirror.

"I may be able to lie to everyone else, but I can't lie to myself."

"All of this is my fault!" Fran said aloud, as she turned to look at William.

With tears in her eyes she continued.

"I caused all of this to happen. It's because of me everything got so out of hand." Becoming so distraught at her revelation, Fran was forced to sit down in an attempt to calm her nerves.

"I should've listened to you, honey. I should've!" she mumbled sadly, as her mind took her back to where her family's vicious cycle began.

"Hello, my name is William. Welcome to the family!" –William

Forty-five years ago, a 17-year-old Fran stood in front of the congregation with her older brother and mother, as the pastor gave a special prayer for the church's newest members.

"Lord, today we come to you, pleading for your mercy and grace, over this young family as they struggle with the loss of their husband and father."

The pastor's prayer soon became muffled to Fran, because she was focused more on staring back at the handsome young man sitting in the third pew, than on what the pastor was asking from God on her family's behalf.

The truth was, Fran's father hadn't passed away, this time nor the other eight times her mother had spoken of his unfortunate demise. Even though she'd never met him, she knew he was living somewhere on the east coast. The whole story was just a ruse to tug at the hearts of the church's leadership and members so the family could get some quick cash with no strings attached.

Fran smiled softly at the young man, and right on cue, she shifted her focus back on the pastor as he said,

"Church, I plead for you all to imagine the hardships this young family is facing now. We are going to have a special offering to help this family out. So everyone, get up and stand on your feet, reach for your wallet or purse, and show them the love we have in this church for those in need!"

As the congregation stood, the musicians started playing loudly and the pastor yelled,

"When you get up here, make sure you shake their hand, give them a hug, and welcome them into our family!"

Fran could tell by the look on her mother's and brother's faces that they were thinking the same thing she was. This was special; no other churches had ever shown so much excitement in helping them out like this one. Member after member ran up and did exactly what the pastor requested. Fran shook so many hands that everyone started to look the same. That is, until she heard a voice say nervously, "Hello, my name is William. Welcome to the family!"

Speechless, all Fran could do was smile as she shook the young man's hand. She watched as he turned and tripped over his shoe laces as he went back to his seat and thought to herself, *William!*

**"Because guys like me don't get girls like you.
We are not even in the same league!"
–William**

"And so by the power vested in me, I now pronounce you husband and wife. You may kiss the bride!"

Two years had passed since they'd first met, and William and Fran found themselves being pelted with dry rice as they slowly walked out of the church's front doors after making the ultimate commitment to each other.

As the limousine pulled away, Fran sat back and closed her eyes. And just as he always did, an attentive William asked as he lightly rubbed her thigh, "Are you okay, baby?"

"Yes, honey, I'm fine. I'm just thanking God for sending you to me!"

A pensive William bashfully smiled as he turned his head in an effort to avoid making eye contact so Fran didn't see him blushing; but it was too late. That is what made Fran fall head over heels for William in the first place. He was nothing like the other guys she'd dated before him. William was a hardworking man who'd just got his dream job. He was very responsible when it came to handling his personal business, and very frugal. William was Fran's genie in a bottle, and he promised to grant all of her wishes.

"It's crazy!" William thought out loud.

"What's crazy?"

"That a woman as beautiful as you are, would consider dating, let alone marry, an average fellow like me! I never told you this, but since we are married I will."

"What is it, baby?" Fran asked.

"When I first laid eyes on you, I immediately felt sorry for myself."

"Why?"

"Because guys like me don't get girls like you. We are not even in the same league!"

"Don't be silly; you are every woman's dream. Everything about you reminds me of my father and for that, I promise to always love you!"

"And I promise to always love and provide you any and everything you want, and be your protector, like your father," William responded with a smile on his face, before leaning over to give his new bride a kiss.

"You promise?" she asked.

"I promise!"

"I just want you to be happy, baby!" –William

Life couldn't be better for Fran. She married her knight in shining armor, whose talent matched his ambition, allowing him to earn his second promotion in just a little over two years working at his company. Fran was the ultra-supportive wife who understood that her role was to support her husband as he focused on moving up the professional ranks, even though it meant she hardly saw William throughout the week. "He's smart. He's handsome. He's positive. He's also a protector, and a gentleman who provides for my every need, from taking care of all the bills, to protecting me from harm."

"If the worst thing that could happen to me is that I get everything I want, then William could work eight days a week if he desires!" is what she always told her friends when they brought up the many hours William spent away from home, leaving Fran all by herself.

One of the promises he made to Fran on their wedding day was that he would always provide her with whatever she desired. And she had done her part to ensure that he lived up to that promise every single day.

One weekend, the couple was invited to a cookout by some of William's coworkers who lived in the next town over. After the cookout ended, the two headed home.

"Now that was a beautiful home, babe!" Fran stated.

"Yeah, the entire neighborhood is amazing," William responded.

"William, what do you think it would take to buy a home like that?"

"I'm not sure, but I know we are a few years away from being able to do that, especially with us just buying our home less than a year ago."

"But babe, how long has he been at the plant, and aren't you his supervisor?"

"He started after me, and yes he does report to me. But, what does that have to do with anything?"

"You're his boss, and he has a bigger and better house than you! That's kind of sad if you ask me."

"I was so embarrassed when I saw the look on his wife's face after I told her where we lived."

"I don't want to over-play my hand, Fran, and struggle financially because I'm trying to keep up with the Joneses," William replied.

Disappointed by his stance on the situation, Fran turned and gazed out of the window to catch one last view of the spectacular neighborhood and said softly,

"But you promised!"

Hearing his wife's last comment, and seeing her energy level decline as the sadness in her eyes increased, a dejected William said,

"I will explore some options tomorrow."

"Are you serious?" Fran questioned in excitement.

"I just want you to be happy, baby!" William replied.

"You're the only man for me. You always know what to do to make me happy. I love you!"

"Love you too!"

"If that calls for splurging a bit, then splurge we will, as long as we are together!" –William

A year had passed since the couple moved into their new home as they walked through the mall, both on cloud nine after receiving some life-altering news.

"Oh, William, this is the perfect dress for our baby's first pictures," Fran expressed with great joy.

"Yes," William replied, "It is beautiful. I can't wait to see it on her!"

After a couple of hours went by, and three more baskets were filled, an agitated William asked,

"Don't you think buying so many clothes and shoes for a baby that will most likely grow out of them before she even has a chance to wear them a second time is going a little overboard?"

"William, this is our little gift from God, and I will make sure she never has to question how special she is to us."

"Yeah, I understand where you are coming from, Fran, but she isn't even here yet."

"Raising her is going to be a marathon, not a sprint, so don't be so impulsive. We don't have to buy everything today."

"Plus, I only budgeted for less than half of what's in the baskets."

The smile Fran had on her face turned to a look of frustration and disappointment at the position William had taken. After a brief moment Fran responded,

"I apologize, William, for wanting our daughter to have the best of everything. From the time I was born, I had to wear the hand-me-downs my brother outgrew because my mother could not afford to buy me new clothes."

"I promised myself that if I ever had a child of my own, that I would do whatever it took, even if I had to sacrifice something, to ensure that he or she would not experience the same hardships I had to go through."

"I figured we were out here already, and since most of the items in the basket are marked down, that it would be no problem buying them."

"But since you make the money, you have final say on how it's spent. So you decide what needs to go back. I don't feel too well, so I'm going to go rest in the car while you finish."

William shook his head as Fran turned to walk out of the store. As she reached the car she thought out loud,

"Shoot, I forgot to get the keys from William."

As she turned to go back to find William, she was surprised at the sight of him exiting the store with so many items in his hands that a store associate had to help him carry everything out to the car. As they drove off after loading the car, Fran asked,

"William, what did you do?"

"After you expressed your feelings to me about your experiences growing up and what you had to suffer through, it made me realize that I was being too rigid in my thinking. I don't want you to stress about anything, so if that calls for splurging a bit, then splurge we will, as long as we are together."

Fran looked William in the eye as she grabbed his hand and said,

"Nothing will ever tear us apart!"

"Plus, I got the television for only twenty more dollars a month." –Fran

With William and baby Melanie gone spending some father-daughter time out on the town, Fran sat on the back porch, sipping on some ice-cold tea, enjoying some down time, when suddenly her peaceful morning was interrupted by the sound of a large truck backing down her driveway.

Wow, they are actually on time, she thought, as she looked down at her watch on her way to the front door. When she opened the door, there were two men standing on her porch. One of them said,

"Good morning, we have a delivery for this address."

"Yes, that is correct, come on in," Fran responded.

After about thirty minutes the men left, and Fran sat down and relaxed on the new sofa that was sitting in front of the new television they'd just delivered.

William suggested that Fran go out and buy a new sofa to replace the old, tattered one they'd had for years. When she went to compare the cost of purchasing it outright compared to renting it, she found that renting it would be their best option because of the low weekly cost, compared to the large upfront out-of-pocket price. Sure, over the long haul they would potentially end up paying more by renting; but figuring she would not keep the furniture through the whole term Fran thought out loud, "Plus, I got the television for only twenty more dollars a month."

"That's the best thing about renting furniture; I can always upgrade or add another item to our account anytime I want, with no strings attached." Feeling a sense of joy from the smart economic decision she'd just made, she thought to herself as she picked the remote control up to turn the television., *I can't wait till William gets home to see what I did.*

"Anything for you, honey!" –William

"Honey, what's for dinner?" William asked, as he walked through the living room after pulling a long and grueling double shift.

"We're meeting the Andersons for dinner," Fran responded, as she walked out of the bedroom.

A physically worn out William responded,

"Really?"

"This is the fourth time we've eaten out this week, Fran. I just want to relax at home tonight."

An upset Fran turned as she threw her arms up in disgust. An alarmed William mustered up enough energy to chase after her down the hall. When he caught up to her, to his dismay, her eyes were filled with tears.

"Honey, what's the problem?"

"Why do you ask, when you really don't care!" Fran responded, to William's surprise.

"What do you mean, I don't care?"

As she rolled her eyes, Fran responded,

"Every day you leave the house and are around adults to pass the time, while I'm stuck at home with the baby all day. When I try to schedule some time to spend with other adults without any children around, you always have an issue with it."

"Fran, I understand how you could mistake me not wanting to go out all the time as me not caring, but that's the furthest thing from the truth."

"It's just that I'm so tired from working all of this overtime."

"Well, that's why I had them make the reservations so late, to allow you to take a catnap if you needed," Fran responded

"Fran, you have to understand that eating out almost every day is depleting our bank account; we just cannot afford it."

"Well, what am I supposed to say when I receive an invitation? 'No, sorry, we can't come because my husband says we're broke.' "How embarrassing do you think that would be?"

A defeated William responded, "All right already, I'm tired of fighting. Let's just go!"

"Maybe after a couple of drinks tonight you will relax. You've been wound up the last few days," Fran acknowledged as she retrieved her coat.

As they pulled up in front of the restaurant, the Andersons were already there, standing in front, waiting for them. Fran turned to William and said,

"Before we get out of this car, you have to promise me that you will try to have a good time."

"Anything for you, honey," William replied in a sarcastic tone as he got out of the car.

"Anything for you."

"What's the big deal? It's just a thousand dollars." –Fran

"Wow, what's that smell?" William asked as he walked in the house after pulling another double shift.

"Yeah, that smell is so fresh, isn't it?" Fran replied

"Whatever it is you used to clean the house with, keep using it!"

With a smile of accomplishment on her face, Fran responded,

"It's not *what* I used, it's *who* I used!"

Not quite understanding the words that were coming out of her mouth, William asked Fran to clarify what she was saying.

"I hired a cleaning lady to come every Friday to clean the house."

"You did what?"

"Why? It's just us, with a baby who can't even crawl yet. What do we need a cleaning lady for?"

"To help me with the major cleaning, that's all."

A disgruntled William responded,

"If you'd just asked me before you made the decision to hire her, I would've told you that hiring a cleaning lady was a huge waste of money."

"How much is she?"

Nervously, Fran answered,

"Two hundred and fifty dollars a week."

A shocked William replied angrily,

"Two what? Are you serious?"

"Tell her you're sorry, but you've changed your mind."

"I can't, William," Fran cried.

"What do you mean, you can't?

"I signed a contract agreeing to retain her services for twelve months, and if I broke the contract, I had to pay a steep cancellation fee."

"Why on earth would you do that without consulting me first? I'm already working a double shift almost every day to handle the obligations we already have, and now you tell me I have to come up with another thousand dollars a month?"

"Fran, all you have to do is a little every day, so the work in the house does not build up; it's that simple."

After taking a deep breath, William announced as he walked out the front door,

"I'll be back. I need some fresh air to clear my head."

As she watched her tired husband stumble out the door, Fran thought to herself,

What's the big deal? It's just a thousand dollars.

"It was a big deal. It was all a big deal!" Fran yelled out, as she turned to check on William as he rested peacefully in the hospital bed.

"What was a big deal? What are you talking about, Ma?" Melanie asked.

She was so caught up in her thoughts, Fran did not hear her family return to the room.

Unprepared at the moment to discuss anything with them, Fran just ran out of the room with tears in her eyes.

William

"Why did I let desperation cloud my judgment into thinking suicide was the only solution?"
–William

William heard the commotion in his hospital room as he slowly regained consciousness.

"Fran," he attempted to call out as she left the room, but because of his critical state, it was impossible for him to raise his voice above the blaring sounds of the machines.

Why? he asked himself.

"Why did I let desperation cloud my judgment into thinking suicide was the only solution?"

What were the courses of action that led my family into the Vicious Cycle? he thought, as he closed his eyes while another tear fell down his cheek.

"More like a bad nightmare." –Fran

"Fran, I'm at wits end!" William announced, as he crumbled up the piece of paper he was reading.

"So there is no other option?" she asked, in a voice sounding more like their daughter than his wife.

"No, there is nothing else I can do. Vandals have damaged our old house so badly with all the graffiti and broken windows that there is no way I can sell it. It's been impossible to pay for two mortgages, even with the overtime I've been working, so I had to make the tough decision and sacrifice one of the houses."

Distraught at the news she'd just received, Fran suggested,

"There has to be something else we can do."

"Have you tried talking with the bank?"

"Fran, I'm so far behind in payments that the bank is no longer willing to hear what I have to say. The letter I just read states that unless I pay the total balance within thirty days, they will foreclose on our old home. And we both know that there is no way I can pay that in that short time frame!"

"I should not have listened to you in the first place when you begged me to move into this neighborhood. I knew buying a bigger home, when we were struggling to pay for the smaller one we were living in, was not a wise choice, especially since we hadn't found a buyer or a tenant to rent it. And now my credit is ruined."

Saddened at seeing a chink in her knight in shining armor, Fran grabbed William around the waist and said,

"Baby, we have a beautiful life. We are healthy, we are in love and happy, we are about to have a beautiful baby and we still have a home to live in. Don't worry about your credit; you have everything you need."

After taking a deep breath, William laid his head on Fran's shoulder and said,

"You're right. We are young; we have time to correct this."

"I have an idea," Fran stated.

"Let's go out for some drinks to help you relax."

"I would love to, honey, but I have an early morning meeting with my boss tomorrow, so I really should be heading to bed."

"A meeting with your boss? Are you getting another promotion or something? You see, I told you, everything is going to be fine."

"I'm not sure what the meeting is about. He just asked me to come in early tomorrow. So don't get your hopes up too high."

"Okay, William, but stop stressing; it's not worth it. The worst thing that could happen with your credit being damaged is we just have to pay cash for everything, and I can think of a lot worse things to go through than that."

William lifted his head from Fran's shoulder and turned to enter the bedroom.

"Sweet dreams!" Fran called out.

"More like a bad nightmare," William mumbled under his breath as he entered the room.

Everything hinges on my meeting tomorrow. he thought, as he pulled an envelope from his drawer and placed it in his briefcase.

"Everything!"

"I guess there is no other option; bankruptcy it is!" –William

It was 7:15 the next morning, and William was already at work. He hated having to work so many long and hard hours, but that was the only way he could quench Fran's thirst for the finer things in life. As efficient and responsible as he was at handling business at work, William was the total opposite at home. He knew Fran was due to give birth to their baby soon, and what they should've been focusing more on was saving money, rather than spending it. But because Fran had whatever money William made spent before it hit the bank account, the couple found themselves living paycheck to paycheck. This was not how William envisioned his life would be, but because he did not want to disappoint his wife, William always conceded and went against his better judgment.

As William sat down to meet with his boss he asked,

"Before we get started, can I ask you a question?"

"Sure, William what is it?"

"You think I can work a couple more weekends next month?"

His boss took his glasses off and looked at William and said,

"You're already falling asleep on the job from all the hours you are working now, and you are looking extremely stressed. So actually, I scheduled this meeting with you to tell you that instead of writing you up and blemishing your impeccable track record, which could potentially ruin your chances at any future promotions, I've decided to cap the amount of hours you work a week to forty."

"But–" William tried to respond before being interrupted.

"Now, William, I am willing to revisit this situation next quarter; but I am forced to leave now, because I have a 7:30 interview coming in that I'm about to be late for."

William watched as his boss left the room. Once the door closed, he took that envelope out of his briefcase and read over it again before burying his head in his hands.

After a few minutes of pondering with his head down, William sat up and thought out loud.

"I guess there is no other option; bankruptcy it is!

"Even though I knew better, I always went against my better judgment and appeased you!" –William

A few years had passed when William stormed into the house and yelled to his wife in an excited voice:

"Fran!"

Startled at the tone he used and not sure what he was calling her for, but could tell that he was not happy, she decided to wait before she answered, to see if she could gauge the situation.

"Fran, where are you?" William asked.

"Yes, dear, I'm here in the back room!"

Her curiosity piqued at what her husband wanted, as a nervous rush of adrenaline flowed through her veins. Fran decided to walk down the hall to meet him halfway. As she turned the corner, Fran could tell he was disappointed by something from the look he had on his face. William extended his arm out to give her the envelope he was holding and asked,

"What the hell is this?"

She grabbed the envelope from his hands and looked down to read what it was that caused her loving husband to become so irate. After scanning over the document inside Fran slowly looked up as she took a deep breath and said,

"I'm sorry."

"You're sorry?"

"That's not going to cut it this time. You promised you would not bail her out, and once again you've lied to me!"

"When Melanie was born, we promised to work as a team and not make the same financial mistakes we made that forced us to have to file for bankruptcy. And of course, as always, you continue to act like a damsel in distress when it comes to something in your mind that you just have to have."

"Even though I knew better, I've always gone against my better judgment and appeased you. I told you that always rescuing Melanie when she mismanaged her money would create a bigger problem for everyone in the end. And now I see you've done it again."

"You paid her overdue car payment, and now our bank account is overdrawn!"

"I've worked hard to repair my credit over the years, and now it seems you are trying to ruin it again!"

Surprised at the tone William talked to her in and the news he just gave her, she asked,

"How is the bank account overdrawn? I checked the balance before I did it."

Frustrated at her irresponsibility William yelled,

"The account is overdrawn because I had to write a postdated check which I dated for yesterday to the store to pay for the furniture you rented!"

"But it's our baby!" Fran responded

"No! This has to stop now, Fran. We can't keep feeling sorry for not being able to give Melanie everything she wanted when she was a kid because I had to file for bankruptcy. We made major mistakes financially and had to pay the price for our lack of discipline. The best thing we can do now for our daughter is educate her about our financial missteps, so hopefully she won't be forced to endure the hardships and pain we had to work so hard to overcome. Our daughter may not have gotten everything she wanted, but she received everything she needed."

"You can't keep going through life as if the bankruptcy never occurred. I can only pray that something bad doesn't happen, because we have no savings or anything put up in case of an emergency. We have no health insurance because I can't afford to pay into the company plan, and I'm not even contributing to my retirement plan. After all that trimming, we are still living paycheck to paycheck because we are not on the same page. At this rate, I will be forced to work until the day I die!"

With tears steadily flowing from her eyes, Fran looked at William and said,

"I'm sorry, baby, I really am!"

"It's just that when I look into Melanie's eyes, I still see that little baby girl God blessed us with so many years ago. And I always say to myself that the two of you are my reason for being, and as long as we all have each other, we can accomplish anything!"

"We will get through this, but if we lost it all today and had to live under a rock, I would still love you with all my heart!"

Touched by Fran's words, William smiled and said,

"You always know the right things to say, and yes, we will get through this."

As William bent down to hug Fran he said,

"To be honest, I can't blame you, because I have the same reaction when I look Melanie in the eyes. Now, what's for dinner?" They both laughed as they headed down the hall into the kitchen.

"She's lived her life recklessly because she knows at the end of the day we will be her life line!" –William

Years later, as he listened intently to his wife finish her conversation with their daughter Melanie, William screamed as she hung up the phone.

"What did you just do?"

"What was I supposed to say? They are all alone, with nowhere to go," she answered.

"Fran, we can't afford to feed four more people, and with us recently downsizing, we have no room for them, either."

"But William, the children need our help. Melanie has done her best to take care of the kids with no help since Scott was arrested, and now she finds herself out of options. My maternal instincts kicked in, and I agreed to something without fully thinking it through."

"I told you years ago, Fran, that always bailing Melanie out of financial jams would only create a bigger problem in the end. She's lived her life recklessly because she knows at the end of the day, we will be her life line. Every time you used guilt as a motivation to provide her with everything she asked for growing up, only caused her to become more unappreciative of things she got. She's never realized that nothing comes easy; you have to work hard for what you want in life."

"Now don't get me wrong, I love Melanie and the kids; but enough is enough. Once again we have to put our financial future in jeopardy to help her."

"She has three months to get her affairs in order, and then they have to leave!"

"But Will—!" Fran started to say, before William abruptly turned and walked away, saying before slamming the bedroom door,

"We are done talking; three months, and not a single day longer!"

"We are too old and too broke to take care of Cindy's kids!" –William

As the years continued to go by, William and Fran continued to find themselves in the eye of one storm after another. After their latest argument, which is what they do more than anything now, Fran stood outside the bathroom door where William had locked himself in.

"William, can I come in?" Fran asked, as she knocked at the door.

"Yes," William answered, in a somber voice.

When Fran entered the bathroom, she was shaken to the core by the sight of her once powerfully built husband, who now bore more of a resemblance to a flower wilting in the hot sun.

"We are too old, Fran, and too broke, to take care of Cindy's kids. I just cannot do it!"

After taking a deep breath, Fran responded,

"With their father not wanting them, the only other option is to put them in the system William, and that would haunt me until the day I die. Melanie and Andrew have already stated that they can't afford to take care of them, and I have not heard from Bobby yet."

"I bet if those selfish pieces of sh—"

"William!" Fran interrupted.

"I'm sorry, Fran but I'm just sick of the spoiled monsters we've created."

"I bet if there was money involved, those scoundrels would be breaking the doors down to get their piece of the pie."

As he tried to finish his thought, William became overwhelmed with emotion.

"Oh, I'm just so sad, Fran, I am just so sad. What are we going to do?" he asked, as he sat on the bathroom floor.

Looking down at her husband, with tears forming in her eyes, Fran said,

"I don't know!"

"I, I don't have insurance!" –William

It had been a few months since the death of his granddaughter Cindy, and William found himself visiting a doctor's office after suffering from shortness of breath and minor chest pains. He'd suffered in silence since the beginning, figuring it was just stress related to all the issues he had been dealing with. But when he fell in front of Fran, clutching his chest as he hit the floor, his secret was exposed.

After being rushed to the emergency room and treated, he was referred to a heart specialist.

Fran held the door for William as they entered the office and walked to the front desk.

"Good morning, may I help you?" the nurse asked.

"Yes, I have a ten forty five appointment."

"Okay, I do not see you in our system. Is this your first time visiting us today?"

"Yes."

"Okay, no problem. I just need you to fill out a new patient form, and also give me your insurance card so I can make a copy."

"Insurance card?" William asked.

"I, I don't have any insurance."

"Oh," the nurse replied.

"If you don't have insurance, then it's the doctor's policy that you pay for your office visit at the time of service."

"What, really?" Fran asked. "How much is that going to be?"

"Well, I don't know that answer right now, because it all depends on what test the doctor determines he has to perform on you today. And that determination cannot be made until he sees you. So you are looking at, at least two hundred and fifty dollars at a minimum, and that's not factoring in any medication you may need."

"What?" Fran screamed. "That's insane; we don't have that kind of money!"

Already physically and mentally worn out from everything he had been dealing with over the past few years, a defeated William grabbed his wife's hand and said to the nurse before turning to leave,

"We'll think about it."

**"Four decades, and not a damn thing
to show for it!" –William**

Less than a month later, as if anything could get worse, William walked down the hall and heard a coworker yell,

"Hey, you take care of yourself now, it's been a pleasure!"

William waved and turned to continue the long walk from the office lobby to his car. Which is something he had done many times before, but over the last few years, has become harder and harder to do. This, however, was a special moment, because it would be his last time doing it.

Because of budget cuts, William's position was phased out. The only option he had to stay employed with the company was to work in the maintenance department, but with his advanced age and poor health, there was no way he would be able to perform his daily duties.

As he reached his car, he turned around with tears in his eyes.

Four decades, he thought

"And not a damn thing to show for it!" he stated out loud as he got in the car and drove off. "Not a damn thing!"

"Your sales pitch is horrible, and you sound like a desperate product pusher looking for a big payout!" –William

"William. William, did you hear what I just said?" Fran asked as a despondent William sat drinking a glass of vodka, unfazed at the news his wife had just given him. Even though he'd heard when she said Bobby had a career-ending injury a few months ago and was on his way back to live with them, he could not help but to focus on his own problems.

He'd spent the last few months looking for a job with no success, adversely affecting his confidence and self-esteem. Every time he saw the worry in his wife's face, he felt less and less of a man, because there was nothing he could do to protect her. Every dollar of his meager severance package he'd had to spend had brought him closer and closer to a zero balance, rendering him more and more unhappy with the realization that there was no way of filling it back up. Sure he got a small pension to live off of, but with the medical bills piling up and the additional mouths to feed, it put them so far in the hole every month that it didn't even matter.

Even though deep down inside William blamed Fran for causing their dire situation and he found himself arguing with her every chance he got, he still loved her immensely, and would give his life for her if he had to.

"William, are you going to say anything?"

"Yes, babe, I heard you. That's too bad for Bobby."

After looking down at his watch, William stood and said as he rushed to grab his coat.

"I'll be back shortly; I'm late."

"Late for what?" Fran asked.

"I'm meeting Andrew for lunch."

"Oh, I'm so happy you two are on speaking terms again. Tell him I send my love."

"Okay, I will,"

William responded, as the door closed behind him.

En route to the restaurant, William thought back to the time Andrew tried to sell him life insurance. Even though he knew the importance of having a safety net in place for Fran in case he died, he just couldn't afford it, and was too embarrassed to tell his grandson about his dire straits.

"Son, life insurance is a great way to make a living, but a huge waste of money!"

Caught off guard by his grandfather's statement, Andrew responded,

"You are highly mistaken, Grandpa, and you're making a huge error not listening to what I have to offer. Just answer a few questions, and I'll tell you what product you need!"

Frustrated that his grandson would not let him off the hook, William resorted to attacking his motives and abilities.

"Your sales pitch is horrible; and you sound like a desperate product pusher looking for a big payout. No one with any financial savvy will ever do business with you until you polish up your delivery."

It really hurt William seeing the damage his words did on Andrew, but he didn't know of any way to get out of not buying a policy; that is, until now.

William looked down at his watch to see what time it was. He had been waiting at the restaurant for more than twenty minutes, and no surprise, Andrew had yet to arrive. After a few more minutes passed, the idea of leaving popped in William's head before he heard,

"Hey, Granddad, sorry we're late," Andrew said, as he and a young lady approached the table.

"This is my good friend Monica that I was telling you about. She will take care of you since I don't have my licenses anymore."

"I will sit here and help with any questions, but I assure you that you are in good hands."

In a strange twist, for a man who'd spent his entire life ignoring the need for insurance, even though he knew the importance, William ended up taken out a three-million-dollar policy. William suspected that Andrew knew that he could not possibly afford the hefty monthly payment, and yet he had proven more than willing to once again take advantage of his ailing grandfather, and facilitate the sale that he was probably getting a cut from. Knowing what he knew about Andrew's legal issues and the tough times he faced, William could not blame his grandson. Besides, William had never had any intention of paying the premiums for long.

"All I have ever done, I did for my family!" –William

It's clear to me what happened, William thought to himself, as he lay in his hospital bed with his eyes closed.

"After all the wrong I've done in my life, my greatest mistake was not in spending frivolously on the things the family desired, but in setting a bad example and passing down my bad financial habits to the next generations."

It was one thing because of bad money management on his part to be forced into work past the normal retirement age. And he was resigned to the fact that as long as he lived, he would be sending whatever little money he had to angry creditors. But the idea that the careless examples he'd set and the negative effects it had on his entire family had sentenced his wife, daughter, and grandchildren to a similar fate, and at an earlier age, no less, had proven too much to bear.

William intended on delivering the miracle his family needed, but the miracle had not ended well. The authorities found William, a man who rendered himself into a bloodied mess, at the bottom of a ravine, trapped inside the crushed shell of the family Lexus. Later that same night, Fran found a note her knight in shining armor left on the dresser beside their bed.

"This is the only deliverance left," the note read. "Please tell Melanie and the kids that I love them. Don't fret over me, Fran. All I have ever done, I did for my family. I die a proud and grateful man. Enjoy the life insurance money."

"He did it all for us and left you with nothing." –Andrew

When his daughter and grandsons' arguing increased, he finally heard Fran's voice as she came in to tell them to be quiet and get out before they woke him up. As she went out to confront them in the hall, William could hear her take a deep breath as she always did when she was readying herself to say something important; but she stopped, because the noise in the hall was even louder than she'd anticipated. Bobby started to yell at his mother, whose hair was so disheveled that she looked homeless. Andrew joined the argument so violently that he looked ready to trade blows. A pair of nurses making their rounds walked by and stared at them in disbelief.

"Enough!" Fran hollered.

Slowly the family quieted down. Fran allowed the peace to settle in before she prepared to say what she felt she must say. But before she could get the words out, Bobby interrupted and told Andrew he should go pick up Cindy's kids from school because no one's home.

That statement launched Andrew into another episode of squabbling. Fran tried screaming again to quiet everyone down, but no one listened. This time, she had to step between her grandsons and physically separate them before anyone paid her any mind. By the time she felt all eyes on her, she was seething. Slowly she became aware that some of the eyes belonged to other families in the waiting area. Her family had made a spectacle of itself. This was no longer a place where she felt comfortable to reveal her news.

"Everyone back into the room," she ordered through her teeth. "There's something I need to share with you privately."

With hanging heads and angry faces, her family followed her back inside. She fired a quick glance at William to ensure that he was still asleep, not knowing he was actually awake because he was lying with his eyes closed. When she felt confident that he couldn't hear her, she offered revelation. She was surprised by the lack of emotion as she informed her family that her husband had attempted suicide in the effort to secure a life insurance payout that would help get their lives back in order.

"But Grams, that's ridiculous," Andrew said in response.

An unexplained fury came to Fran's heart. "Your grandfather's unconditional love for you is not ridiculous. Don't you see what this means? He was willing to sacrifice himself to save all of us. Can you imagine anything more selfless... more—"

"It's stupid is what it is," Andrew interrupted.

Fran gritted her teeth as everyone shifted their attention to her eldest grandson. Andrew shrugged in a way that suggested an apology, but his eyes said something different. His eyes looked almost like he relished this moment.

"There's a two-year suicide clause in Grandpa's policy," Andrew announced to everyone's dismay. His face assumed a strangely con-spiratorial look as he also announced, "Plus, when I helped sign him up with the insurance policy, I discovered that Grandpa had selected the single life payment option from his pension when he retired. If he dies before you, Grams, there won't be anything left for you. All of the money he is receiving monthly dies with him."

Silence fell over the family. Fran felt a frantic sorrow creep into her throat. Where before she had been resolute, now the tears came.

"He did it all for us, and left you with nothing!" Andrew said.

To her horror, Fran turned toward her husband to find that his eyes were open. From his wide eyes and chalky pallor, it was clear that he had heard every word. For the briefest moment, she saw her same sorrow reflected back at her from him. But quickly, the sorrow was replaced with fear. The steady beep of the heart monitor picked up its pace. William clutched at his chest. Fran rushed to her husband's side. The heart monitor bled into a slow, continuous ring. William's eyes clenched shut. Fran called out to him. She felt her family crowd around them, everyone staring down at the man who had so loved them as to give them life and end his own.

"William?" Fran said softly, desperately.

William's tension slackened. His hand fell from his chest. His head lolled to the side. The heart monitor droned on with a continuous beep.

THE END

Epilogue

Sadly, the story you just read is a realistic example of what can happen when you mismanage your finances. Don't be discouraged though, because with hard work, dedication, and discipline, not only can you get out of the vicious cycle, you can prevent your children from going through it as well!

Follow these steps to avoid any financial pitfalls that could come your way, but remember; it's just a start. Everyone's situation is unique, so after reading this book, whether you have a one dollar or millions of dollars, consult with a qualified and trustworthy advisor to ensure that you and your family are on the right path to financial security.

Single Adults:

Living on your own will create its own set of challenges, from responsibly managing your finances to the purchase of your first home. Believe it or not, this phase of your life could potentially be more stressful than you'd ever imagine. Here are a few tips to help you get on the right path to financial independence.

1. Create a budget and stick to it.
2. Start an emergency fund to handle the unexpected.
3. Start saving for retirement.
4. Understand your taxes.
5. Get a health insurance policy if you don't already have one.
6. Live below your means.
7. Protect your credit.

Married Couples:

Finances are one of the most problematic areas in a marriage. The earlier in the relationship couples focus on getting on the same page financially, the better. Here are a few tips to help you to begin planning a long financially happy life together:

1. Communicate, Communicate, Communicate, and adapt as needed.

2. Develop a joint financial dream list.

3. Schedule weekly business meetings to go over household bills and other business that affects your household finances.

4. Live below your means.

5. Save 20 percent of your after-tax income now. (Including 401(k) savings, contributions to a defined benefit pension, etc.)

6. Take care of your credit.

Retirement Planning:

Financial security in retirement takes planning, commitment, and the most important thing: **money.** Unfortunately, less than half of Americans have calculated the amount they need to save to live comfortably during their retirement years. With the average American living 20 years in retirement, it is important to start as early as you can in preparing for that monumental day. If you have not started, you are not alone; but start now, because the longer you wait, the harder it gets. Here are a few tips to help you to begin planning for your retirement:

1. Ask questions so you can fully understand your retirement needs.

2. Start saving, continue saving, and stick to your plan.

3. Don't touch your retirement savings.

4. Contribute to your employer's retirement plan, such as a 401(k).

5. Find out about your Social Security benefits.

6. Take care of your credit.
7. Consider basic investment principles.

Professional Athletes:

Professional athletes are highly talented individuals who often make headlines for the multimillion dollar contracts they sign. Unfortunately, a high percentage of the same athletes we celebrate become bankrupt or experience financial distress shortly after, and sometimes before, their careers end. In 2009, *Sports Illustrated* estimated that 78 percent of NFL players went bankrupt within two years of retiring. It was also shared that an estimated 60 percent of professional basketball players were bankrupt or financially broke within five years of retiring. It seems incomprehensible to the average person when they hear how quickly someone can go from millions to poverty, but it happens every day.

Here are a few tips to help you begin planning for success after you hang them up:

1. Understand your contract, and what you are truly getting paid after taxes   and other fees are calculated.
2. Do not let your friends or family members manage your money.
3. Form a trustworthy team of advisors to assist you with ALL financial decisions.
4. Remember, it's not what you make, it's what you keep.
5. Get an insurance policy to guard against risk.
6. Take care of your credit.

Single Parent

Single parents are multitasking machines that tend to the many jobs that have to be done to keep the family unit healthy and happy. Between the homework help, the cooking, the laundry, and the many birthday parties, family finances are easily overlooked. For single parents, it can be especially difficult to find the time to devote to long-term financial planning, yet doing so is critical to ensuring the prosperity of your family. Here are a few tips to help you begin planning for financial success as a single parent:

1. Keep track of your income and spending.
2. Get life insurance.
3. Protect yourself with disability insurance.
4. If you are uninsured, get health insurance.
5. Set up an emergency savings fund.
6. Take care of your credit.
7. Create a Will.
8. Choose a trusted Guardian to take care of your children.

Dual Parent Household:

Having two parents in the household is a little easier than being a single parent raising the children by yourself, but it still has its challenges. I could easily combine the two sections into one because the same tips I gave in the single-parent section apply to this section as well, and vice versa.

We hear about new lists released every day about how to be a good parent to our children. Some of the examples given are as follows:

1. Express love and affection to your children.
2. Praise your children.
3. Avoid criticizing your children.
4. Be a role model for your children.
5. Spend quality time each day with your children.

While the five keys to being a good parent I just listed are good, there is one piece of advice constantly left off the many lists, but is just as important as the others.

Teach your children how to manage their finances when they are young!

And I don't mean it's a **do as I say not as I do** situation. Being a good role model in handling your finances will not only make the family unit stronger, it will save you and your loved ones from the kind of heartache and struggles we witnessed the Johnson family dealing with in the book. It reminds me of a poem my mother had hanging in the kitchen when I was growing up:

CHILDREN LEARN WHAT THEY LIVE
If children live with criticism,
They learn to condemn
If children live with hostility,
They learn to fight
If children live with ridicule,
They learn to be shy
If children live with shame,
They learn to feel guilty
If children live with encouragement,
They learn confidence
If children live with tolerance,
They learn to be patient
If children live with praise,
They learn to appreciate
If children live with acceptance,
They learn to love
If children live with approval,
They learn to like themselves
If children live with honesty,
They learn truthfulness
If children live with security,
They learn to have faith in themselves and others
If children live with friendliness,
They learn the world is a nice place in which to live.

The world may have been different when Dorothy Law Nolte wrote this poem way back in 1972, but as you see, some things are still the same. There was no focus on early financial literacy. If I was able to add a line to the poem it would be:

If children live in a financially stable household,
They'll learn to be financially responsible.
TEACH YOUR CHILDREN EARLY!
Join my movement - Break the Vicious Cycle of Financial Illiteracy.
You can follow me, tweet me, like me or email me:
My blog: Bruce-wayne.me
Twitter: @bruceprosperity
Facebook: Bruce Wayne Breaking the Vicious Cycle
Brucewayne2197@yahoo.com

Made in the USA
San Bernardino, CA
19 January 2017